How to Write the Best Research Paper Ever!

by

Elisabeth Blandford

authorHOUSE®

AuthorHouse™
1663 Liberty Drive
Bloomington, IN 47403
www.authorhouse.com
Phone: 1-800-839-8640

First published by AuthorHouse 8/11/2009

ISBN: 978-1-4389-0949-3 (sc)

Printed in the United States of America
Bloomington, Indiana

This book is printed on acid-free paper.

CONTENTS

RESEARCH PAPER FOR ENGLISH STUDENTS

Philosophy for Students

The foremost goal of the research paper project is to learn the processes of researching and composition. At this level, it is most important for you to develop the skills necessary to produce the paper, primarily the reading, understanding, evaluating and connecting of ideas from material that is more sophisticated, complex, and perhaps more technical than what they have done before.

Additionally, you are going to develop life-long skills of organization and persuasion, using the various methods of writing which correspond to higher level thinking skills, and writing with methods such as definition, exemplification, cause and effect, comparison/ contrast, classification and analysis, and ultimately, synthesis.

Furthermore, you will be exposed to the use of a standardized convention for writing that has very specific requirements which you must learn and to which you must adhere.

Moreover, to be successful, you must make and keep short and long-term goals. You ultimately have to make an ethical decision on some controversial topic on which you have become somewhat of an expert. The exciting result is that you become your own teacher, making decisions on what you will learn, when and at what pace you will learn it, and how you will express it. For some students, this is the first time you will actually be the director of you own curriculum, which is very empowering.

INTRODUCTION

The Research Paper is taught conforming to a timeline. It encompasses up to ten weeks of work in the classroom. The process is rife with composition and reading assignments. Peer Conferencing, as well as style, summary and paraphrase exercises give many listening-speaking opportunities.

As for thinking skills, the material presented in the book itself is quite challenging, but also the thinking an individual student does in the process of completing the paper is extraordinary! The use of higher level critical thinking skills of analysis, evaluation and synthesis is abundant. You will have many opportunities to infuse creative thinking skills, such as originality, flexibility, fluency, imagination, curiosity, elaboration, risk-taking and complexity into your work.

The research paper process in this book is presented in a step-by-step approach, with each step giving an opportunity for one or more graded assignments. You will have the chance to rewrite each part of your papers as you go along. You truly learn the process and skills, improve your grade, and ultimately produce a finer end product. Rewriting your work will have more meaning for you, and have a longer lasting effect. Thus, this curriculum is designed for success with each assignment, small or large.

The information in this book is based on the *MLA Handbook for Writers of Research Papers, 7th edition*. Copies of it are available in most libraries and bookstores; it will be an invaluable resource.

WHAT TIME IS IT? IT'S A TIMELINE

Have you ever sat down to a dinner that included something you hated? You knew you had to eat it; there was no dog to slip it to, and no place to hide it on your plate. Ah, the old quick bite and a swallow of milk trick, right? What about this: Have you ever wanted to be great at some game or sport, but then realized that you would have to learn a lot of different little skills and strategies before you'd be good enough to play it? Well, writing a research paper is much like these two situations. Some of the work may not appeal to you at all, but if you do it one little step at a time, you will find that you can do the whole project. Some of the skills and strategies may seem difficult because they are new and challenging, but they are achievable, and once you have them, they'll hold you in good stead forever.

One of the hardest concepts to see at first is the importance of TIME. Once you see the scope of the assignment, however, you will realize how much time you really need to do a better than adequate job. Thinking, searching, reading, evaluating, organizing and writing takes time! Therefore, you should follow a step-by-step process over an appropriate length of time, in order to do everything excellently.

Here is a basic timeline, which will show you many steps.

Week One:	View a presentation board that represents a sample paper
	Preview the textbook
	Discuss goals of the project
	Define research and plagiarism
	Preview Spelling and Vocabulary words
	Read a sample paper and its outline
	Brainstorm and choose a topic appropriate for the assignment
Week Two:	Learn how to narrow the topic to fit the assignment
	Begin a list of questions you have about your topic
	Learn how to do a Works Cited List
	Do Works Cited Exercise One (practice for your own Works Cited)
Week Three:	Learn to use Library Resources
	Use the *Reader's Guide to Periodical Literature* in the classroom
	Visit the School Library
	Use the school computer lab for online research
	Begin a Working Bibliography
	Read with a new purpose
	Learn how to summarize and paraphrase sources

	Practice summarizing
Week Four:	Practice Paraphrasing
	Learn how to parenthetically document sources
	Visit other local libraries, such as city, and/or nearby college or university library
	Add to Working Bibliography
	Gather sources
	Read and highlight sources; take notes
Week Five:	Gather sources
	Learn how to write a Thesis sentence
	Learn how to write Functional Introduction sentences
	Write and Peer Conference Thesis and Functional Introduction
	Read and highlight sources; take notes
Week Six:	Learn what a Hook is
	Learn how to build the Introductory Paragraph(s); write and submit
	Learn how to Write a Formal Outline
	Learn how to handle opposing evidence
	Learn how to build a Preliminary Outline; write it
	Read and highlight sources; take notes
Week Seven:	Turn in Preliminary Outline
	Learn and discuss logic and fallacies for drawing conclusions
	Learn and discuss methods of writing development: exemplification, comparison/contrast, cause and effect, definition, categorization, analysis and synthesis
	Learn appropriate methods for Concluding
Week Eight:	Review Works Cited requirements; Do Works Cited Exercise Two
	Write a Sentence Outline
	Learn techniques of Writing Style: word choice, transitions, tone
Week Nine:	Learn how to create a display board on the topic of the paper
	Learn typing, pagination and spacing requirements
	Write the Works Cited for the paper
	Write the Rough Draft of the paper
Week Ten:	Peer Conference the Rough Draft
	Self-evaluate the paper
	Revise and Edit
Week Eleven:	Publish two copies of the Final Paper.
	Create a display board for class exhibit
	Celebrate!

GOALS AND OBJECTIVES FOR STUDENTS

To choose a topic of personal curiosity and value that will sustain interest over ten weeks

To effectively and efficiently use library resources and technology to gather information

To evaluate information from gathered sources and construct a knowledgeable thesis

To recognize connections and relationships between research resources

To gain confidence in one's own opinions

To recognize and organize major and minor supporting evidence for the thesis

To recognize opposing evidence, present it adequately, and maintain stronger evidence in support of the thesis

To develop flexibility in changing a judgment or viewpoint

To present ideas logically and in a variety of developmental methods to persuade a reader to agree with the thesis

To develop logical Preliminary and Sentence Outlines

To write, use, and correctly parenthetically document summaries, paraphrases and direct quotations from sources

To use transitional markers and devices to connect ideas smoothly and logically

To recognize fallacies of logic and draw logical conclusions

To write a rough draft from an outline

To learn to proofread, revise and edit one's own work

To produce a polished, clean product

To evaluate the development, organization and style of a classmate's work in order to become a better self-critic

To keep to a timeline and successfully do a long-range assignment

To direct and control a path of learning to achieve self-set goals

THE RESEARCH PAPER: A DEFINITION

What is a research paper? It is not a report that lists lots of facts from encyclopedias. It is not an essay that expresses your opinion on a subject. Actually, a research paper is a combination of both. In the research paper, you will logically use facts and statistics and examples about your subject which you have found in a variety of sources, from libraries--books, magazine and newspaper articles, pamphlets, reference books, videotapes--and from other sources, such as interviews and non-fiction television shows you watch and record. You will use all this information to develop an opinion about your subject, and then use the evidence from your sources in your paper to persuade your reader to agree with you. There are special ways to introduce your evidence so that your reader knows you have gotten it from authorities, and that you didn't make it up yourself. It is crucial that you clearly document (record) the sources of all your information because not doing so is dishonest and unethical. Using other peoples' work without giving them credit is a form of cheating called PLAGIARISM. There are several ways to ethically write about information that are logical and interesting. This book is designed to teach you the step-by-step process of researching and writing the paper that results from your work.

What is research? It is a lot of work! Researching is a long, time-consuming process that takes desire, dedication and determination. It can be fun and funny, exhilarating, frustrating and satisfying. You must select a topic you care about enough to work on for nine or ten weeks. The process includes the development of many higher level thinking skills and important study skills that will last you for the rest of your life, even beyond school and college! Since you will be writing on a topic different from everyone else's, you will truly be in charge of your own curriculum, and your own learning. That's really exciting, and it can be kind of scary, too. But we all begin the same way. Here are the required materials for the project: three ring binder, loose leaf paper, dividers, two different colored highlighters, pens and pencils. The Divider sections shall be: Loose leaf, Working Bibliography, Articles, Notes, Questions, and TILT (Things I Learned Today), which is a place for personal reflection.

Here are the steps, in a nutshell . . . all 31. Now you are ready to start the real work!

To successfully write the research paper, you have to [1]plan and [2]follow a timeline; then, [3]brainstorm and [4]choose a topic; [5]narrow it down to something specific enough to fulfill your assignment; decide what you [6]initially think you want to prove about your topic; [7]question what you know and [8]don't know; use [9]library materials and technology to [10]gather information; [11]photocopy sources so you maximize your library time in gathering information (you can then read these sources anytime, anywhere); [12]list all your complete documentation for your sources; [13]read as much as you can; [14]highlight and [15]write notes on your photocopies; [16]evaluate what you have read and learned; [17]create your persuasive (thesis) statement; [18]select what evidence you want to use; [19]organize what you have selected in an outline; [20]write the rough draft using [21]summary, [22]paraphrase and [23]direct quotes with [24]correct documentation; [25]polish your paper with transitions and [26]style; peer conference with a [27]partner or [28]two; and finally, [29]edit and [30]revise before you [31]publish your paper. WHEW!

So, where is the essence of *you* in this paper?

You probably recognize that your research paper is going to contain many ideas from a number of authors. In fact, most of the paper will be made up of direct quotes, summaries and paraphrases of evidence, examples and illustrations from your many sources. That disturbs some writers because they cannot see where the opportunity comes in for *their original ideas. Your original work and ideas are very subtle,* because you must NEVER use the word "I" in your research. You, as the writer, should never appear obvious in the paper. Anytime you write "I believe," or "I will explain," or "in my paper, I. . ." or 'I think that . . ." or "in this report," you are weakening the strength of your authority. It sounds very childish to use any of those introductions. How can you be a knowledgeable, sophisticated authority if you sound childish? Also, you need to be direct and get on with your paper; after all, it's going to be long enough without your saying that you are about to say something. Just say it, see? Think Nike and just do it! You will want to state everything as fact. If you make your reader think it is only your opinion, it is not as convincing.

OKAY, SO WHERE ARE **YOU**?

So just where are **you** in your paper? Actually, your originality is everywhere! It is in your choice of topic, in your creation of an interesting, thought-provoking introduction, and in your thesis sentence that expresses your unique opinion. You are in your choice of which authorities to use, in your logical arrangement of evidence based on your judgment of what is most important, and in your use of transitional language to smoothly move your reader from one idea to the next. You are there in your choice of words that will express your style and tone, and in your method of concluding persuasively. And finally, your originality is expressed in your integrity, which comes from fulfilling your obligation to make all your ideas and their connections clear to the reader, and to document the authorities you use according to accepted convention. This book uses the *MLA Handbook for Writers of Research Papers, 7th edition* for its standards of convention.

SPELLING AND VOCABULARY

The following is a list of terms and their definitions, organized in the chronological order of the research process.

1.	research	the use of multiple sources and authorities to study, question, and write about a specific topic—either to discover and publish information, or to persuade an audience to agree with a persuasive thesis concerning that topic
2.	topic	a subject of study
3.	essay	a written composition that promotes an opinion
4.	plagiarism	an act of using someone else's thoughts or words without giving them due credit, thus, representing their work as your own. Plagiarizing is a form of cheating by stealing.
5.	organization	the method by which information is ordered logically
6.	timeline	a calendar of events and assignments due for the project
7.	periodical guide	an index of articles published in periodical journals and arranged alphabetically by subject, title and author
8.	citations	ordered information of sources used in writing the paper, following a specific convention (MLA, in this case) that identifies each source by author, title, and publication, etc.
9.	abstract	a summary of an article found with the citation information, used by researchers to determine whether or not the article itself will be useful; it cannot be used as a source by itself.
10.	synopsis	another word for abstract
11.	highlight	to mark a written source with a colored, transparent marker that emphasizes pertinent information a researcher wishes to remember or use in writing
12.	Library of Congress	a classification system used by libraries to organize books
13.	Dewey Decimal System	another classification system used by libraries
14.	duplicate	to make a copy

15.	Works Cited	an alphabetical list of sources (by last name) used in writing the research paper, organized by a specific convention (MLA, in this case), placed at the end of the research paper, but starting on its own new page, numbered consecutively
16.	indent	to start a new line one tab from the left martin (approximately 5 letter spaces) on computer, or one inch in handwriting, to signify a new paragraph, or to create white space, as in an outline (showing a breakdown of categories going from most general to most specific), or in a Works Cited
17.	bibliography	a formerly used title for the Works Cited, meaning "list of books." Because we can use many other sources than books (such as interviews, recordings or Internet), the new title Works Cited is used.
18.	development	the way in which information is put together in a specific logical order (see words 29—38.)
19.	summarize	to report the main points of information in the same order as presented in a source, usually one-third to one-quarter the length of the original, using different terms than the author's
20.	paraphrase	to retell, perhaps translate, information from a source, specifying all information given, but in words different than the author's, and often using more words in which to do it
21.	focus	to concentrate on one thing
22.	notes	information written on a photocopy of a source, or perhaps on note paper, which sifts out the most important information given, or statistics, or quoted material, which the researcher wants to remember, use, or can connect to another source; it can be an inference or an evaluation
23.	thesis	the most important sentence of the research paper, the thesis presents an educated opinion on the topic, which is written clearly, concisely and persuasively, and represents a "contract" between the writer and reader/audience that indicates the writer's intent to provide evidence in a logical manner
24.	Functional Introduction	a mini-outline of the entire paper written in sentence form, which lays out the intended subtopics in a logical order, the Functional Introduction is found in the introductory paragraph of the paper, along with the thesis sentence and a hook, which is information designed to grab the reader's attention

25.	Preliminary Outline	an outline, following the order of the Functional Introduction, of the subtopics and sources that will be used in much more detail in the actual research paper, designed to lead the reader smoothly from one point to the next in persuading the reader to agree with the paper's thesis
26.	outline	an organized, written map of the paper in its "skeleton" form, detailing the content's order and going from most general to most specific, using an alternating format of numbers and letters, and corresponding indentations to signify divisions (Roman Numeral, Capital Letter, Arabic Numeral, Lower Case Letter)
27.	parenthetical	within parentheses
28.	documentation	names, titles and page numbers that identify exactly where specific information originated, that precisely match the sources as they are listed in the Works Cited
29.	comparison	showing the similarities between things, ideas, events
30.	contrast	showing the differences between things, ideas, events
31.	exemplification	explaining or illustrating a point by using examples
32.	cause	something which initiates or provokes something to happen
33.	effect	the result of a cause
34.	illustration	a written image; use of words to describe
35.	narrative	a story written in chronological order using specific details
36.	descriptive	information which is detailed and specific that may appeal to the senses
37.	analysis	the breakdown of something into its contributing parts
38.	categorization	the placement of things into similar groupings
39.	transitions	words and phrases used to promote an even, smooth flow of one idea into the next, such as conjunctions, and words which show a logical connection or order
40.	tone	word choice (diction) and punctuation used to reflect the attitude of the writer toward the topic
41.	style	the writer's way of expressing thoughts, depending on diction, tone, and variety in sentence length
42.	pagination	the way in which page numbers are located on a page
43.	conclusion	a logical inference, or a generalization drawn from evidence; also the ending of a paper
44.	evaluation	a judgment of something's value or worth

45.	peer	a person who is a colleague, an equal
46.	conference	a discussion, written and/or spoken, about a specific topic
47.	proofread	to read over one's own work, or another's work, marking errors in expression, style, grammar, spelling, capitalization, punctuation and development
48.	revision	to rewrite a paper by changing the content, adding or deleting, and/or changing the order of information
49.	edit	to correct errors in mechanics and grammar
50.	success	achievement

TOPIC, TOPIC: TO PICK A TOPIC

For some people, when given the chance to write on anything they would like, the assignment is as clear as spring water. They know exactly what they want to research and write—it is as if they have been just waiting for someone to give them the opportunity to try. For others, the assignment is as clear as mud. Some people just aren't sure what to do with such a free assignment; they can't think of a topic, and then they worry, and the worry becomes panic and panic becomes paralysis. They are stuck. If you are stuck, take heart! There are good ways to get unstuck.

One way to get unstuck is to remember part of the definition of a research paper. Your purpose is to use information that you gather to persuade someone to agree with you about something. Do you have a strong opinion about a controversial subject? A controversial subject has more than one possible way to reasonably view it. That might be a place to start. List several controversial subjects you have heard or read about at school, at home, or in the news lately. Write the topic, the controversy and your opinion.

TOPIC   CONTROVERSY   OPINION

_____

_____

_____

Are any of these controversies researchable? Will you find enough information on them to support a paper the length of your assignment? Do you care about any of these topics? Are you interested enough in any one of these controversies to work with it for ten weeks? If you answer yes to these questions about one of these subjects, you probably have a good choice for your paper. But here is a word to the wise. You must be prepared to be flexible. The tricky thing about controversial subjects is to avoid stereotyping and prejudice. Sometimes we think we know how we feel about a subject, but once we start digging into the facts of it, we find out we didn't know enough, and we were wrong about it. If you are able to change your mind and write a paper from the other side of the argument where there is clearly more logical evidence, then do so! You won't have to change your topic, just your opinion. If there is only a small amount of opposition to your opinion, there is a proper way to include it and maintain your point of view. It is discussed later in the book.

TOPIC, TOPIC: TO PICK A TOPIC (continued)

But if you cannot accept the opposing information, you would be better off changing topics completely than trying to write a paper that will clearly be unsuccessful due to a preponderance of evidence against you.

If trying to find a controversy doesn't work, try this way. List below subjects that you know more than just a little about. They could be things you've learned about in school, or at home, or in your hobbies, sports, friendships or your everyday life. Then decide if there is anything controversial or challenging about the subject. Is there anything related to laws or rules? Is there anything unfair about the subject?

TOPIC   CONTROVERSY   OPINION

_____

_____

_____

A third way of finding a topic is to ask yourself what topics you would like to know more about, but have never had the time to study. Are there any controversial aspects about those subjects? Do you have an opinion on them? List them here.

TOPIC   CONTROVERSY   OPINION

_____

_____

_____

A fourth way to find a topic is to list your favorite things. Perhaps out of that list you can find an idea you can develop into a research paper. List your favorite things below. Is there anything controversial about them? Why do you like them?

TOPIC   CONTROVERSY   OPINION

_____

_____

_____

Once you have come up with some good ideas that you might want to pursue, share them with your classmates in a giant brainstorming session. Remember that a good brainstorming session can't occur if kids think they might be laughed at; every idea has merit. Take a risk and share yours. One of the great things about brainstorming with a big group is that you can get a lot of ideas.

Another good thing that you should try to make happen is to build on each other's ideas. If you think of something to make an idea bigger or better or more specific, well, let everyone know! Don't be surprised if you end up changing your topic choice after brainstorming. When students work together and create better, more complex ideas that result in a more elaborate and successful project, that is called synergy. GO FOR IT!

TAKE YOUR TOPIC ON A DIET: NARROW IT DOWN!

Once you have chosen a topic, you have to decide how to narrow it down or limit it in order to 1.) fit the assignment's length ; 2.) be appropriate to the assignment; and 3.) fulfill the purpose of the assignment. Your teacher will guide you in all three respects.

One way to narrow down or limit a broad topic is to determine if there are subtopics, or certain categories within a broad topic. Take, for instance, the topic DRUGS. That is an interesting but huge topic. Ask yourself, what are the different kinds of drugs? Then fill in a WEB diagram to help you see that you still have many choices as you narrow down or focus in on your subject. Look at the following example.

LEGAL		DEVELOPMENT OF DRUGS	
alcohol	prescription	generic	orphan drugs
nicotine	over the counter		animal testing
accidentally addictive	purposely abused		

ILLEGAL DRUGS	
recreational use	drug trafficking

From this web, you can then write lists of ideas for each category, such as:

Alcohol	Accidentally Addictive	Orphan Drugs
teen alcoholism	sedatives	funding
Alcoholics Anonymous	painkillers	Who needs it?
Fetal Alcohol Syndrome		
Drunk Driving Laws	**Purposely Abused**	**Illegal/ Recreational**
MADD/SADD	steroid abuse	LSD, Marijuana, PCP
Just Say NO programs	athletes	heroin, cocaine
Educational programs	animals	Diseases associated with AIDS
Nicotine	**Generic Drug Development**	
premature births	economy	**Drug trafficking**
smoke hazards	research capabilities	smuggling
heart/lung diseases	insurance incentives	federal government
cancer	**Animal testing**	legislation
insurance rates	moral?	DEA
fire hazards	alternatives?	International drug Cartels

QUESTIONS, QUESTIONS: WHAT DO YOU KNOW? WHAT DON'T YOU KNOW? WHAT DO YOU WANT TO KNOW?

You must have chosen your topic because you are interested in it. But you probably chose your particular topic because you already know some things about it. Good! That gives you a starting place. A really good way to get and stay motivated about your paper is to constantly ask questions— of yourself, of other people, and of the research sources available to you. Research is a little like the private detective business; the more questions you ask, the more there are to ask! When you finally have asked and answered all of your questions, you will be ready to start writing your paper. Keep a list of the questions you have, and add to it as you proceed. Another advantage of generating a list of questions is that it will help you stay on your topic.

The following questions are often referred to as The Reporter's Formula because they are designed to get all the important facts a reporter would include in the first paragraph of an article. They are a way of just getting to the facts. Answer these questions about your topic to help you see what you already know.

Whom does this involve? _____

_____

What is this? _____

_____

What is important about this? _____

_____

When does/did this happen? _____

_____

Where does/did this happen? _____

_____

Why does/did this happen? _____

_____

How does/did this happen?_____

_____

Here are some other questions that are perhaps more specific about your topic.

What are the problems involved in this topic? _____

_____

_____

What other topics is this related to? _____

_____

What moral issues surround this topic? _____

_____

What is dangerous about this topic? _____

_____

What are the laws that affect this topic? _____

_____

How much money will it cost to fix this problem?_____

_____

Where will the money come from? _____

_____

What will be the arguments against my opinion on this topic? _____

_____

What will be the arguments for my opinion on this topic? _____

_____

Now add your own questions _____

_____

DESSERT FIRST . . . OR LET'S START AT THE END! HOW TO CORRECTLY MAKE A WORKS CITED LIST

Psst! Do you want to know a secret that can save you hours of unbelievable frustration from having to do the same job over again? Although it's not ice cream, here's the scoop. The last page(s) of your paper will be an alphabetical listing of all the authors and publication information of the sources you use. It is called the Works Cited. People used to call this page the Bibliography, but that term is outdated. It means a list of books. In research now, we use many more kinds of sources that aren't just from print, for instance, videotapes of news broadcasts, phone interviews, and the Internet. Thus, the title of this information in your research paper will be more accurately described as Works Cited.

This section of your paper proves that everything you write came from an authoritative source. Remember, you don't want to plagiarize.

So, right at the beginning of your research, as you start to gather titles of sources and their authors, you should find out and list all the required information about each. Thus, the end of your paper will be easy to do correctly! This preliminary list is called the Working Bibliography because you will continue to add to it during the whole research process, as you find new material that is pertinent to your work. For two reasons you must include all the required information about each source that you want to read or examine. The first reason is to enable you to more easily find that source on the Internet, in the reference section, the magazine stacks or on microfilm in your local or school library. The second reason is to create a list for yourself of all your sources' credentials for the later preparation of your Works Cited page. Can you imagine not writing down that information the first time you see it? You would have to go back to get it all over again, which would be incredibly frustrating. Instead, be efficient!

The Working Bibliography may end up being quite a bit longer than your final Works Cited, for you may discover when you scan a particular source that you thought was going to be, say, the icing on your cake, that it is indeed unusable, not even food for thought. That's fine. Many people, once they get the hang of locating sources have so much fun at it that they quite exceed what they need for their paper. A ball park target for a Working Bibliography of a paper that should end up being seven to ten pages long, could easily be a list with 25 to 50 entries. From it you may end up only using 10 to 15 sources in your paper. That's okay! You don't have to use them all, just as you really don't have to eat all the treats on the dessert cart, but they are nice to look at!

On the following pages you will find general and specific criteria for citations in the Works Cited. Study the examples and take the text with you to the libraries so that as you record information about sources, you will get everything that is necessary. In your visit to the school and public libraries, you will discover that the order of bibliographic information is not the same as the order of information in the periodical guides, and also not the required order for using the MLA Convention! Put them in the correct order *as you record them*. There are three forms in the section entitled Working Bibliography. Photocopy them to use and keep in your binder. Following the examples of Works Cited entries are two exercises that will help you appreciate the trickiness of this job!

PREPARING THE LIST OF WORKS CITED

General Guidelines

As you write a research paper, you must indicate exactly where you found any and all materials you borrow—whether facts, opinions, or quotations, summaries or paraphrases. You should acknowledge your sources in the text of your paper by placing the author's last name and the page on which you found the information in parentheses, thus keying each documentation to its complete citation in your Works Cited. Although this list will appear at the end of your paper, you should make a rough draft of it as you research and enlarge your Working Bibliography as you add sources. This way you will know what information to give in parenthetical references as you write, whether you are using note cards, writing on Xerox copies, outlining, or writing your rough or final draft.

Placement

Remember, the list of Works Cited is like dessert; it appears at the end of the paper. Just as we clear the dinner plates and then serve the cake, the Works Cited starts on its very own page, numbered consecutively after the last page of your text. Thus if your research paper ends on page 10, the number on the Works Cited page will be 11. Look at the Works Cited pages by Raymond after the following page for examples of spacing, placement and indenting.

On every page of your research paper, place the page number in the upper right-hand corner, one-half inch down from the top of the paper, preceded by your last name, as in all the previous pages of your paper. The number should be flush with the right hand margin. The title of your page must read Works Cited. <u>It must not be underlined, it must not be made bold, it must not be inside quotation marks, and it must not be in all capital letters. The title is centered, and placed one inch from the top of the paper.</u> Double space and begin the first citation flush with the left-hand (one inch) margin. Continue to type across the page, but do not type into the right-hand margin (one inch). If the entry extends beyond one line, double space again, and then indent the second and any subsequent lines of that entry five spaces (one inch, if handwritten) from the left-hand margin. This method of indenting creates a white space around the authors' names, making it easier to see them distinctly. Continue to double space between and within each entry throughout the entire Works Cited. **The double spacing between lines should remain constant throughout your whole paper.** Continue the Works Cited on as many pages as necessary, numbering them consecutively—11, 12, 13. The title Works Cited is necessary only on its first page.

Arrangement

- The entire Works Cited should be alphabetized by the authors' last names.

- If there is more than one author for a source, you should alphabetize by the first author mentioned; DON'T alphabetize the names listed—*whichever author is mentioned first is mentioned first for a reason*; perhaps she or he did the most work!

- Alphabetize by the letter-by-letter system. MacDonald, Roberta, comes before Maldonado, Isidro which comes before Malvasio, Frank.

- If the author's name is unknown, then alphabetize by the title of the article or book, using the first word in the title other than A, An or The.

- If the title begins with a numeral, alphabetize the title as if the numeral were spelled out. For example, "1,000 Ships Launched" will be alphabetized as if it began One thousand.

- If you use two or more articles written by the same author, alphabetize the citations by the name of the article or book. In such a case, you would use the author's name in the first entry, but you would not repeat that author's name for the second or third. Instead, at the beginning of the second entry, type three hyphens followed by a period (---.); then space twice, and type the title.

> Let's say you are using three books in a series of six by the same author and with identical titles except for numbers; do not organize the entries by chronological order. <u>Stay alphabetical</u>. Hence:

> Cecconi, Tyler. *Alien Encounters: Part Five.* New York: Hardy Press, 1988. Print.

> is followed by

> ---. *Alien Encounters: Part Four.* New York: Hardy Press, 1987. Print.

> is followed by

> ---. *Alien Encounters: Part One.* New York: Hardy Press, 1984. Print.

More specific examples follow for the most typical sources you will use. If you have a source for which there is no information, consult the *MLA Handbook for Writers of Research Papers, 7th Edition.*

WORKS CITED

Aguero, Marimar. *"Update What We Read."* Letter. *The Journal Times* [Racine]

    14 Apr. 2006: B2. Print.

Allen, Diamond. *"Learning Reading and Writing* by Talking." *Teaching K-8* 124 (2007):

    531-35. Print.

Anderson, DeShawn and Christian Jackson. *"The Fragile World of Pleasure Reading."*

    English Journal 234.7 (2001): 85-87+. *Ebscohost.* Web. 6 June 2009.

Baumann, Michael, Cody Reynolds, and Nick Dismore. *Why Adults Read: They*

    Learned as Children. Chicago: Cook County Press, Ltd., 2001. Print.

Berry, Dylan and Ryan Strausser. *"All about adolescent literature: Pro and Con."* Journal

    of Reading 212.5 (2004): 76-78. *LexisNexus.* Web. 20 Jan. 2009.

Brown, Quanisha. *"Cooperative Learning Affects our Business Life."* *Group Work in the*

    Classroom. Ed. Tim Pape. San Diego: Harcourt, 2006. 8-18. Print.

Carter, Brytanie. Personal Interview. 22 Jan.2005.

---. *"A Study of the Ability of Secondary School Pupils to Perceive the Plane Sections of*

    Selected Solid Figures.": Diss. University of Wisconsin-Madison,1966. Print.

Clark, Drew, et al. *Read!* Madison: U of Wisconsin, 1996. Print.

Comstock, Luke and Brenton Heckel. *"Changes in Some School Literature Classes."* Time

    27 June 2006: 56-8. *Time.* Web. 8 Aug. 2008.

Fanning, Aaron and Matt Knudson. *"Curriculum Changes Setting School Board on Edge."*

    The Journal Times [Racine] 28 Oct. 1996: B1. Print.

Gordon, Elizabeth and Anthony Shuman. *"Creative Responses Make for Lasting Memories." Atlantic Monthly* 29 May 2007: 56+. *Ebscohost.* Web. 28 Oct. 2008.

It's a Wonderful Life. Dir. Frank Capra. Perf. James Stewart, Donna Reed, Lionel Barrymore, and Thomas Mitchell. RKO, 1946. Film.

Jensen, Leslie. *"Young Adult Lit a Major Breakthrough in Middle School Classes." Academic America.* 13 Aug. 2006. *Google.* Web. 2 Aug. 2009.

Morelan, Jeanette. *"Moving in the Classroom Keeps Transescents Awake."* Encyclopaedia *Britannica.* Encyclopaedia Britannica. 2008. Web. 19 Dec. 2008.

Monti, Ashely, Dir. *"Strangers with Many Faces."* By Ariana Flores. *Children's Television Workshop on Air.* PBS, Milwaukee. 6 June 2006. Television.

"Responsive Reading." *Merriam-Webster's Collegiate Dictionary.* 10th ed. 2004. Print.

Schulz, Susan and Jessica Pfeiffer. *"Welcome to Repeat City."* Editorial. *Chicago Sun Times* 19 Apr. 2006: B17. *Ebscohost.* Web. 5 Mar. 2008.

Welch, Janice and Ryan Saldivar. *"Study Power: Get Organized!" New York Times* 7 May 2009: C27. Print.

RULES FOR AND EXAMPLES OF WORKS CITED STYLES

For all entries, the **first general rule** is that the citation is divided into four categories, always separated by periods:

Author's name. Title of the book or article. Publication information. Publication Medium (Print, Radio,etc.).

The **second general rule** regards <u>underlining</u> versus *italicizing* titles of books, periodical names, newspaper names, names of plays, films, television and radio programs, record albums or cassettes, CD's, operas, musical compositions, paintings, sculptures, buildings, spacecraft, ships or aircraft. Although many computers now generate *italics* easily, for papers that will be graded or edited, the typestyle must be crystal clear. Sometimes italics do not clearly show enough of a difference from the other typestyle. Discuss this with your instructor, and by showing an example of your italicizing capability, gain approval to use it; otherwise, use underlining. In either case, be consistent throughout the paper!

The **third general rule** is that you must continue to double space within and between entries. See the examples below.

1.   A BOOK WITH ONE AUTHOR
      (PAMPHLETS ARE CITED IN THE SAME MANNER AS BOOKS)

To cite a book by a single author, type the author's last name first, comma, space, first name and any middle name or initials as seen on the title page of the book. Follow the name with a period and two spaces. Then type the title of the book, italicize or underline it, and follow it with a period and then two spaces. If the title has a subtitle, follow the title with a colon and type the subtitle, which will also be underlined. Then put the publication information in this order: city of publication followed by a colon (:). Only give the name of the first city if more than one are listed. If the city is not in the United States, list an abbreviation for the country if it is unfamiliar to you or your reader. Follow this with one space, then the publisher's name, followed by a comma, a space, and then the year of the publication, followed by a period. Then type two spaces and the medium in which it was presented (such as Print, Web, Radio, Television). Here is a sample:

Stolzoff, Tara. *In the Middle: Writing, Reading, and Learning with Adolescents.*

   Portsmouth: Boynton/Cook Publishers, 1997. Print.

2.   A BOOK WITH TWO AUTHORS

Do not change the order of authors' names; they are listed in the order they chose, which probably indicates the amount of work done by each. Start with the last name of the first listed author, comma, space, first name (and any middle name or initials) space, then the word "and" and then the name of the second author in regular order, followed by a period. Finish the citation with the publication information as above, in Number One. Here is a sample:

Lopez, Maria and Gabrielle McNeal. *Drama the Arne Totdahl Way*. Milwaukee:

    Adam SanSouci Press, Ltd., 2006. Print.

3.   A BOOK WITH THREE AUTHORS

Start again with the last name of the first listed author, comma, space, first name (and middle or initials) followed by a comma. Then list the second name in regular order, followed by a comma, space, the word "and," and a space connecting it to the third name in regular order. Then type the publication information as detailed above. Here is a sample:

Platt, Silver, Maria Ingersoll, and Sharnesia Stevens. *The Middle School Musical:*

    Melodrama in Every Heart. Chicago: Harcourt, 2005. Print.

4.   A BOOK WITH MORE THAN THREE AUTHORS

If there are four or more authors of a book, only use the first author's name, in reverse order as detailed above; follow it with a comma, space, and then the Latin words "et al," which mean "and others." Finish the citation with the publication's information as above. Here is a sample:

Flores, Rico, et al. *Growing up with an Older Sister*. Chicago: CRivas Press, 2002. Print.

5.   TWO OR MORE BOOKS BY THE SAME AUTHOR(S)

Since both books have the same author, you will alphabetize the entries based on the first word of the title of the book, excluding A, An, or The. Cite the author's name in the first entry only. For the next entry, instead of the author's name, type three hyphens, followed by a period, then two spaces, then the book title italicized or underlined. If the person named is not an author but an editor or translator, place a comma and one space after the name, followed by the appropriate abbreviation (ed. or trans.). If there are two authors, follow the directions for Number Two, above, for the first entry; then follow the directions for using the hyphens. Here is a sample in which the choice is made using "for" before "in," alphabetically.

Couillard, Nicole. *Teaching Literature for the Adolescent*. New York: Columbia

    University Press, 2006. Print.

---. *Teaching Literature in the 21st Century*. New York: Baldwin, 2007. Print.

6.   A BOOK WITH AN EDITOR(S) (no author listed)

List the editor's name as you do an author's, followed by a comma, a space, and the abbreviation ed. (or eds.), and then follow with the regular publication information. Here is a sample:

Johnson, Brody, and Shanina Johnson, eds. *Dictionary of Italian Literature*. Westport:

Greenwood, 2005. Print.

7.   A BOOK WITH NO AUTHOR OR EDITOR

If there is no author or editor listed, form the citation beginning with the title, and follow it with the usual publication information. You will alphabetize this citation in your Works Cited by the first letter of the first word of the title, not including A, An, or The. Here is a sample:

Dictionary of Ancient Greek Civilization. London: Meuthuen, 2001. Print.

8.   A WORK IN AN ANTHOLOGY

If you are citing an article, a poem, a song, a short story, or an essay found in a collection or anthology, you need to add the following information to what you would give for a book entry. Begin with the author of the article or essay, etc. and the title, in double quotation marks with the period enclosed. (However, if the piece was originally printed as a novel, independently, you must underline it.) Next, type the anthology's title and italicize or underline it and follow it with a period. If there is an editor or compiler or translator, type the appropriate abbreviation followed by a period, a space, and the person's name in regular order. Then type the regular publication material: the city of publication, colon, space, the publisher's name, comma, space, and year of publication, followed by a period, two spaces, and then finally, the page numbers of the piece you are citing. Here is a sample:

Lincoln, Abraham. "The Gettysburg Address." *The Elements of Literature, Level 8*. Ed.

Blanca Montes-Rivera. New York: Holt, 2004. 543-44. Print.

9.   AN ENCYCLOPEDIA ARTICLE WITH AUTHOR

Use the same procedure for the author's name as listed for a book. Do not cite an editor. The title of the encyclopedia article is placed in double quotation marks with a period before the final double quotation marks. Follow this with two spaces, then, if the reference book is a familiar one, place the name of the encyclopedia or dictionary, italicized or underlined and followed by a period. For less familiar reference books, you should include the full publication material. If the source material in the reference book is arranged alphabetically, you do not need to include the volume and page numbers. Finally, enter the year the edition was published and the abbreviation ed.

Tuttle, Thomas J. "Baseball's Greats." *Grolier's Sports Encyclopedia*. 2002 ed. Print.

10.   AN ENCYCLOPEDIA ARTICLE WITH NO AUTHOR.

Begin with the title of the article and follow with publication material as above. Alphabetize these types of citations by the first word of the title of the article, barring the words A, An or The. Here is a sample:

"The X-15: Research at the Edge of Space." *The Realm of Science*. 2002 ed. Print.

11.   A MAGAZINE ARTICLE WITH ONE AUTHOR

Use the same procedure for the author's name. The title of the article is placed in double quotation marks with the period before the final double quotation marks, which are followed by two spaces. Then type the name of the magazine and italicize or underline it, **BUT PLACE NO PUNCTUATION AFTER THE TITLE OF THE MAGAZINE.** Now type the date of the publication in the European method (which you will use throughout your paper) starting with the day (no comma) space, then the month (abbreviated to three letters with a period following, except May, June and July) followed by a space (no comma) and the year followed immediately by the colon (:) and then one space. Finally, type the page number(s) with no abbreviation such as p. or pp., (no p'ing in the paper!) and end with a period. If the numbers run consecutively, such as page 8 to 15, type 8-15. If the pagination skips to another part of the periodical, you may type 8+. End with the publication medium: Print. Here is a sample:

Garcia, Josefina. "Romeo and Juliet Again?" *Time* 23 Oct. 2006: 27+. Print.

12.   A MAGAZINE ARTICLE WITH TWO OR MORE AUTHORS

Follow the same procedure for two or more authors of a book in listing their names. Follow the information in number 11 regarding the title of the article, the name of the magazine, the date and page numbers and publication medium.   Here is a sample:

Carson, Cargine and Gage Lueke. "What every senior should know about applying to

college, and why." *US News and World Report* 15 Nov. 2007: 96. Print.

13.   A MAGAZINE ARTICLE WITH NO AUTHOR

Begin with the title of the article. Alphabetize this citation using the first word of the title of the article, not including A, An or The. Continue the citation as you would an article with an author. NOTE: Some magazines are only published on a monthly basis, so no date would appear before the name of the month. Here is a sample:

"The Starry Sky." *Odyssey* Jan. 2004: 26-7. Print.

14.   AN ARTICLE IN A SCHOLARLY JOURNAL

A scholarly journal is generally aimed at professionals who wish to read the latest research and data regarding a specific subject. Most scholarly journals publish four or six issues per year, and are not generally found at the newsstand, but are subscribed to by individuals and libraries. You will undoubtedly find some of your research in scholarly journals. Some of these continue the paging of each issue from the year's first issue to its last, and this generally comprises one "volume" of the journal, which is given a number; the volume numbers progress from one year to the next.

The citation first includes the author's name in reverse order, followed by a period and two spaces. Next, type the title of the article in double quotation marks, the period going inside the last double quotation marks. Next type two spaces and then the publication information, which includes the italicized or underlined title of the journal, a space, the volume number of the journal, period, the issue number, a space, and place the year of the publication in parentheses, followed immediately by a colon. After the colon, type one space, and then type in the page numbers and a period. End with the publication medium. Do not use the words or any abbreviations of "volume" or "issue." The placement of these numbers indicates this information. Here is a sample:

Sisouvong, James. "Learning Reading and Writing by Talking." *Teaching K-8* 124.8

(2007): 531-35. Print.

James, Anna. "Engineering Reflections and Projections: The Life of a U.W. Female

Engineering Student." *Applied Engineering* 123.7 (2004): 36+. Print.

15.　　AN ARTICLE IN A NEWSPAPER

Begin with the name of the author(s) in the usual manner, followed by a period and two spaces. Then type the title of the article in double quotation marks, and enclosing the period. To use a source from a newspaper, you must use the proper name of the paper as it appears on its front page. Do not add the word "The" to its title if it is not there. If the city's name does not appear in the title, add the city in square brackets [ ] after the underlined or italicized newspaper name. For nationally published papers you need not add the name of the city. Next type in the date (European fashion), abbreviating the months to three letters except May, June and July. Do not list the volume and issue number of the paper, but if an edition is mentioned on the front page, add a comma after the date, a space, and the abbreviation of the edition. Follow the date (and edition) with a colon, a space, and the page number, including the section of the paper. Finally, end with the publication medium. Here are samples:

Kiesler, Arianna. "Tennis Outlook." *Journal Times* [Racine] 10 Aug. 2006: B2. Print.

Gutierrez, Cesar. "Navy Intelligence Reels Under Pentagon Pressure." *The Washington*

Post 30 Dec. 2007, late ed.: D1+. Print.

16.　　AN EDITORIAL

Start with the author's name in reverse order, as usual, followed by a period and two spaces. Type the editorial's title in double quotation marks with the period inside the last, followed by two spaces. Next type the description, "Editorial" which should not be in quotation marks or underlined. Follow with a period, two spaces, and conclude with the usual publication information. If the editorial does not list an author, start with the title and continue with the description and publication information. Here is a sample:

Allen, Keanna. "Enforce Drunk Driving Laws." Editorial. *Journal Times* [Racine] 16 June

2006: A7. Print.

17.   A LETTER TO THE EDITOR

Here, use the descriptor "Letter" after the author's name and follow the directions for number 16. A sample follows:

Partida, Fernando. Letter. *Journal Times* [Racine] 18 June 2007: A7. Print.

18.   AN INTERVIEW

There are at least three kinds of interviews. One is a personal interview you conduct yourself. A second kind is one you see or hear, and record from TV or the radio. The third kind is a published interview. First type the name of the person being interviewed, last name first, as usual, followed by a period and two spaces. If you conducted this interview, next give the kind of interview, Personal Interview or Telephone Interview, immediately followed by a period and two spaces. Finally record the date of the interview, in the European fashion. If the interview is recorded or published, after the interviewee's name, type in double quotation marks the title of the interview, if there is one, with a period inside the double quotation marks. If the interview was published independently, italicize or underline it instead. If there is no title, then use the descriptor Interview after the name. Do not underline, italicize or put this description in quotation marks. Finish with the appropriate information on the source, whether it was found in a broadcast or in a book or magazine. Here are samples:

Vonberg, Zach. Personal Interview. 6 June 2006.

Gosa, Kaneen. Interview with Sam Donaldson. *ABC News Tonight*. ABC. WLS,

      Chicago. 5 May 2007. Television.

Obama, Michelle. Interview with Shane Peterson. *Ladies Home Journal* May 2008: 56-9.

      Print.

19.   A TELEVISION PROGRAM

With one exception, every item in this citation is separated from the others with a period. Begin with the title of the episode or segment in double quotation marks, with the period before the last double quotation marks. Next type and italicize or underline the title of the program/series, followed by a period, then name the series, if it is part of one, but without quotation marks or underlining. Next type the name of the television network, followed by a period. Next type the call letters of the local station, followed by a comma, and then the city of the station, followed by a comma. Add the date of the broadcast in European fashion, and end with the publication medium, Television. If one individual is primarily responsible for the broadcast, insert that person's name and descriptor after the program/series title. Here is a sample:

"Ulysses S. Grant." *Civil War Journal*. Narr. Kierra Stills. Dir. Nick Kemen. PBS.

      WTTW, Chicago, 20 Jan. 2006. Television.

20.   A FILM OR VIDEO RECORDING

Begin with the name of the film or video, underlined or italicized and followed by a period. Include the name of the director, the distributor and the year in which it was released, and the medium in which it was seen. You may also add other information that you think is important, such as the stars, the writer, and/or the director. These should be placed between the title and the distributor of the film. If you are referring primarily to one person's contribution, you should begin with that person's name. Here is a sample:

Apollo 13. Dir. Ron Howard. Perf. Tom Hanks, Kevin Bacon, Bill Paxton, and Ed Harris. MCA

   Universal, 1995. DVD.

21.   ENTRIES IN THE WORKS CITED FROM THE WEB

In a Works Cited entry that uses information from the Web, include as much information as is given from the Internet in the following order, each part followed by a period, with ONE exception: #5, the sponsor/publisher is followed by a comma. Use these rules for a citation found Only on the Web (not in print).

1.   The author's name (or editor, or compiler), last name first, with appropriate abbreviation, if any, such as comp. for compiler, followed by a period and two spaces.

2.   The title of the article (poem, short story), followed by a period, all within double quotation marks, and followed by two spaces.

3.   The title of the Website, italicized.

4.   The edition or the version accessed.

5.   Sponsor or publisher of the site. If there is none, type N.p. (No publisher).

6.   Date that the information was posted/published. If there is none, type n.d.

7.   Medium of the article/information posted (Web)

8.   The date that you accessed the article/information on the Internet (dd, mm, year).

   NOTE: When you parenthetically document source materials from the World Wide Web, include information that guides your reader to the correct Works Cited entry. Since web documents frequently do not include page numbers, omit numbers from the parenthetical documentation. If the source does include page, paragraph or section numbers, include those numbers with the appropriate abbreviation, p., para., or sec. Do not use page numbers from a full text (HTML) printout of a web source as its pagination varies from printer to printer and thus is not uniform.

   Bishop, Caleb, ed. *Mark Twain's "The Mysterious Stranger." Newsweek.* Newsweek,

1 Sept. 2006. Web. 2 Dec. 2007.

Use the following rules if a work cited online is also been published in print.

Present citation as it would appear as a print publication, but instead of using "Print" as the publication medium, add the following:

1. Web site or database italicized

2. Medium used (Web)

3. Date of access in European Fashion.

Centeno, Jessmarie. "Managing Today's Inner City Classroom."

NEA Today 4.1(2007): 23-27. Ebscohost. Web. 15 Sep. 2007.

Demet, Paul. "Chocolate Icebox Cake." Gourmet 18 Aug. 2006. LexisNexus. Web.

19 Dec. 2007.

Parker, Shannon. Interview with Alexis Gonzalez. Publisher's World. Nov.

2005:32. Google. Web. 14 Feb. 2007.

Tuttle, Thomas J. "Baseball's Greats." Grolier's Sports Encyclopedia Online.

2002 ed. Google. Web. 12 Feb. 2009

WORKS CITED EXERCISES

CREATE A WORKS CITED LIST for each of the following two sets of unedited and unpunctuated titles and other information given in the sentences below. Arrange them in alphabetical order by last name, or if none, by the title. Write down the rule and their page numbers to help do the work. Do each set separately as a Works Cited page. Put your last name and the page number one-half inch from the top edge of the page and one full inch from the right edge. Then, center the title Works Cited one full inch down from the top edge of the page. Use the correct one inch margin on both sides and the bottom. **Do not number your entries.** Double space within and between each entry, and indent the second and any subsequent line of each entry five spaces if typing, or one inch if handwriting.

Exercise One

1. Stages of Reading Development, by Sarah Perez, was published by McGraw-Hill in New York in 1983.

2. Zoe Herbrechtsmeier wrote an article entitled Ability Grouping: A Tool for Educational Excellence that appeared in the 1993 volume number 168, issue 7 of The College Board Review on pages 20 through 27. You found it online through LexisNexus on August 18, 2009.

3. Richard C. Sprinthall and Norman A. Sprinthall edited Educational Psychology: Selected Readings published in 1969 by Van Nostrand Reinhold Company in New York.

4. Analysa Saenz and Ravneet Randhawa wrote an article printed in Newsweek on November 15, 1993, on page 67. It was called Failing the Most Gifted Kids. You found it through Ebscohost on the Internet on May 27, 2009.

5. Alexis Matsen, Taylor Timler, Breanna Vasquez and Viancka Lopez collaborated on an article about their school play in their school newspaper, The Viking Review, printed in Racine, Wisconsin, on February 13ᵗʰ, 1996. The article was named Little House of Horrors a Huge Success!, and was printed on page 4 of section B.

6. Yilena Vasquez wrote a pamphlet: Life as a Pom-Pom Girl, published by Mitchell Press, Ltd., in 1995 in Milwaukee.

7. Janette Sanchez' novel The Boy Who Reversed Himself was included in an anthology of sci-fi thrillers called Unbelievable Voyages, compiled by Rhea Riley and published in Chicago by McGraw-Hill in 1988. It is found on pages 221 to 398.

8. Yilena Vasquez wrote a pamphlet: Baby-sitting Tips in the 90's, published by YMCA Publishers, Inc., in New York in 1992.

1.   Kyrin Cunana submitted an entry for the *American Encyclopedia*'s 9th edition on AIDS Awareness in the Public Schools. It was published in 2004.

2.   The Challenger Explosion: Its Effects on NASA was printed in the 6th edition of the *Encyclopedia Britannica* in 2005.

3.   Logan Reid authored an article in the *English Journal* titled "Comparing *Taming of the Shrew* to *Much Ado About Nothing*." It appeared in the November/December issue of 2006 on pages 73-96. It was accessed online through *Ebscohost* on April 1, 2009.

4.   Michael Yang wrote a letter to the editor of the *Milwaukee Sentinel* on March 17th, 2007. It was on page B3.

5.   Rashawn Bumpus authored an article published in the *Yale Law Journal*, volume 268, issue number 4 in 2005 called Doctors Suing Doctors on pages 346 and 397.

6.   Kristian May collaborated with Dustin Pfeifer on a research project in 2007. Their essay on its results was published in the *U of Chicago Medical Journal*, volume 112, issue 7 on pages 65-72. Its title was Effects of Ultra Violet Rays on Lifeguards with Blond Hair and Fair Skin.

7.   Editor Jericho Knapik-Christiansen's Sunday, May 8, 2006, column focused on The Rights of Baseball Fans, published in the *Burlington Times* in section A on page 8.

8.   Caoilfhonn Taggart gave a personal interview on September 19, 2001.

9.   Bart's Revenge was the title of an episode of *The Simpsons* aired on FOX in Milwaukee on WTMJ on December 19, 2005. It was directed by Ryan Kaun.

10.   Photojournalism in Kansas is the subject of an article in the *Hawkeye Review* on page C4, by Kristina Jones on June 6, 2006. It was posted on *America Online* on November 22, 2007.

USING LIBRARY RESOURCES—THE SEARCH BEGINS

Now that you have thoroughly prepared yourself to keep accurate records of your source material, it is time to go find your sources. (At last!) Your first stop should be your school library, in which you will probably find reference books indexed in an online computer catalog, along with a selection of newspapers, pamphlet files, audiocassettes, videocassettes, filmstrips, and maps. You will also find magazines, for which there may be at least two possible indexes. Reference books are an important background resource. However, since it takes at least a year for a book to be published after it has been written, you cannot expect to find the most recent information on your topic there. But the information found in reference books is a great foundation on which to build your research. Depending on the dates when they were produced, the other resources may also be really helpful. However, the most current information comes from magazines and newspapers. To be on the cutting edge of your topic, unless it is historical, you will want to focus a good amount of time on those.

School libraries used to carry an abridged version—red covered (and some carried the unabridged version—green covered) of the *Reader's Guide to Periodical Literature*, which is an alphabetical listing by subject and authors of magazine articles. The abridged version lists magazines found in most school libraries. The unabridged version is found in larger libraries, such as public libraries and university libraries. That was back in "the old days." Now, *The Reader's Guide to Literature* is found with multiple other indices through major Search Engines, such as Metasearch 101, which searches multiple engines. Instead of getting the best results one search engine has to offer, you'll be getting the combined results from a variety of engines, such as industry leading engines including Google, Yahoo! Search, Live Search, Ask.com, About, MIVA, LookSmart and more. EBSCOHOST offers a broad range of full text and bibliographic databases designed for research. Subject areas include: academic, biomedical, government, and scholarly journals. Even dissertations and theses published through ERIC can be accessed through EBSCOHOST. This database is accessed through fee-paying libraries, so you may not be able to use it from your home computer, but you may be able to use it through your school, public, or university library computers. One of the best features about some databases, such as those accessed through EBSCOHOST, is that articles from magazines originally published as hard copies can be immediately obtained online, either as just the text (HTML) and/or as "PDF," which means you will see onscreen a picture of the magazine page itself, including any photos or graphics. It is always wiser to use a PDF version because you can get accurate page numbers from those articles when you cite information from them. With HTML, you will not be able to cite any page references that are accurate to the original article. Because your computer may have different font and size settings, the text could be seen on one page, or two or more, but appear differently on someone else's computer screen due to different font and size settings. Page numbers would only represent the number of pages of recorded text, not the actual page numbers of the article as originally printed. With HTML, your citations cannot be as exact as with PDF; therefore, you should always select PDF when it is available.

In your school computer lab or online at your own home, you can research your topic in several valid ways. But first you should know that NO CHAT room is considered a reliable source of information; it is merely a place for an exchange of anonymous, unsubstantiated opinions. You can, on the other hand, undoubtedly find websites that generate accurate, authoritative information using typical commercial search engines, as those mentioned above. The problem in using websites found in those internet sources is that the information may be biased; use caution—substantiate your information with another source.

Here are some additional reliable search engines:

Alltheweb.com	SirsDiscoverer.com
Altavista.com	NY Times Learning Network.com
Ask.com	Studentnewsnet.com
Askforkids.com	GaleOpposingViewPoints.com
Google images.com	

The websites accessed through these search engines provide indexes of journal and periodical articles. They are arranged in date order, listing the most recently published information first. When you have limited your search to specific indexes and put in your search term, you will find options for things such as the dates which you wish to search, and other search terms you wish to use. Get the most recent information!

WORKING BIBLIOGRAPHY

You must keep a complete bibliographic record of each source you use. So when you are even just looking, you should write it all down. That was the reason that the Works Cited section came first in this book, before researching. Now you know exactly what you need.

Different conventions require different kinds of information, and in different orders. Here are three samples of Working Bibliography sheets, arranged according to the MLA Convention for use on your visits to the libraries (one for books, one for articles, and one for the Internet). You may photocopy these pages. You can also create your own forms to include other types of sources, such as interviews, letters, articles from newspapers, etc.

If you do go to more than one library, you should indicate for yourself in a separate column the name of the library, or an abbreviation of it, where you found your source information. If you need to see it or get it again (hopefully you won't lose anything, but if you do . . .) this record should allow you to retrieve it again easily. The forms that follow are recorded in the order required for citations arranged for use with the MLA Convention, 7th Edition. The information you see online may not be recorded in the required order for an MLA Works Cited, so recording your source information on these forms will put you one step ahead later, when you write and organize the Works Cited for own your paper.

Working Bibliography for Books

WB	Author	Title	Place Published	Publishing Company	Year	Library
1						
2						
3						
4						
5						
6						
7						
8						
9						
10						
11						
12						
13						
14						
15						
16						
17						
18						
19						
20						

Working Bibliography for Magazine/Journal Articles

WB	Author	Title	Journal	Date	Vol/iss	Pages	Library
1							
2							
3							
4							
5							
6							
7							
8							
9							
10							
11							
12							
13							
14							
15							
16							
17							
18							
19							
20							

Working Bibliography for Internet

WB	Author	Title	Database	Date posted	Date accessed
1					
2					
3					
4					
5					
6					
7					
8					
9					
10					
11					
12					
13					
14					
15					
16					
17					
18					
19					
20					

ARE YOU THINKING, "OKAY, I HAVE A LOT OF CITATIONS FOR SOURCES ON MY WORKING BIBLIOGRAPHY . . . NOW, WHAT DO I DO?" GOOD!

1. Read through the citations of sources on your Working Bibliography and determine which ones look like good possibilities for use in your paper. Highlight the citations you want to pursue.

2. Most libraries will list their holdings online; otherwise, go to the library's reference desk to see a list of their holdings. Don't waste time looking for something that is not there! Usually several copies of the holdings are available. Reading through these holdings lists either online or in hard copy is the quickest way to see if that particular library owns a hard copy of the magazine(s) you want. Sometimes the listing will indicate that the magazine is on microfilm or microfiche; sometimes it will indicate that only certain dates of that magazine are held. Sometimes the library will not have the paper copy, but will have it online in PDF and/or HTML editions.

3. Mark your chart to indicate if the source is available there; give an abbreviation for the name of that library. If you run out of time, you'll know how profitable your time will be at each library if or when you return. It will also serve as a back up record for you in case you lose some information or need more.

4. Check to see if the magazines you want to look at are out on the shelves available to you. GET THE ARTICLES! If the magazines you want are held behind the library's reference desk, fill out a call slip to give to the librarian who will get the magazines you want. Write legibly and provide all necessary information.

   If you find a source online, but the libraries available to you do not own it, *don't give up*! Libraries participate in networks for sharing materials. Go to the Reference Librarian and request an Interlibrary Loan Form. You will need to fill out the form with all the bibliographic information, and information about yourself, such as name, address and phone number so the library can contact you when the material arrives. The librarian will then search for your source among all the libraries in the network (usually it is the entire state's public and university libraries), request a copy of it, and when it arrives, you will be notified to pick it up. Usually there is a nominal fee, such as five cents a page. Obviously, it is important to identify the sources you need to obtain this way early in your search, as the turn around time is usually ten days to two weeks.

5. Scan the articles to determine if you really want to pay for a copy of them for your binder. Some articles will be useful "hits" and you will want them, but some will be "duds" not worth the time or money.

6.   Make copies of the articles you want.

7.   Use a three hole punch (carefully, so as not to lose information) on your articles so that you can store them safely in your binder.

8.   Place the articles in your binder. You could arrange them by subtopics, using dividers for organization, or you could arrange them alphabetically by author in preparation for doing your Works Cited.

9.   Follow the directions for reading articles on the next page: **Be a Spider!**

READING ARTICLES: BE A SPIDER!

Reading for information you want to use in a research paper is not the same as reading a novel, nor is it like reading from a sociology book for a test. This reading requires you to use your mind in a more complex way. Instead of just enjoying your reading, or learning facts, you will be *evaluating* what you read as you read it. You will be judging its worth to you. You will be *comparing and contrasting* one article with another. You will be *analyzing* (breaking down into parts) information and categorizing it. You will be reading and using definitions. Ultimately, your job as a research paper writer is to take all this information and *synthesize* it (that is, create something new from several sources) into a persuasive argument. So your job of reading for this assignment has new challenges which you will probably like, because finally, you get to create something and have an audience for what YOU think and what YOU want to say!

Have you ever watched a spider in its web? After the spider has carefully tied so many strands together, she is able to catch what she wants and needs: food. If you become a spider in your reading, as you read articles and tie them together with strands of your highlighting and note taking, you will have what you need: all the information to make a persuasive paper. **SO BE A SPIDER!**

1.   Read each article one time just to understand its content, and flavor, and decide if it has worth for you. Decide if you will reread it and set it aside, or junk it.

2.   Read each article a second time. Don't read the same article three times in a row. Go on to new articles so that you can make the connections like a spider. As you read each article and become more familiar with its content, the connections will become more readily apparent. Remember: whatever your articles say to confirm each other's value, the more power you have to support your opinion and so your should record them all.

   A.   First use a **<u>yellow</u>** highlighter to mark things you want to use in your paper

            (there is a reason!).

            1.   Highlight important ideas

            2.   Highlight new ideas

            3.   Highlight statistics

            4.   Highlight quotes

   B.   Underline with a pen to stress highlighting

   C.   Write notes in margins

1.   Make connections to other articles/authors

2.   Evaluate the worth of the information in relation to your thesis

3.   Explain its significance to your opinion

4.   Look for and mark the O, WOW's to possibly use as your hook (see page 73).

5.   Decide, now, while you are most familiar with the information, how best to present it in your paper. It will save you time. Be efficient!

     a. Write an S for **Summarize** this

     b. Write a P for **Paraphrase** this

     c. Write DQ for **Directly Quote** this

The following section on taking notes will explain how and why to use Summary, Paraphrase, and Direct Quotes.

3.   The third time that you read articles, use a **blue** or a **pink** highlighter. If you highlight the same information twice, it will appear **green** or **orange**, signifying that it has great importance to you! Let a simple thing like color help you to organize your thoughts and materials.

On your photocopies, you can use different colored highlighters to code certain subtopics. Some people write notes to themselves in the margins of the copies, such as "This is exactly what I need!" or "This author agrees with so-and-so (another author)--so it strengthens my point!" Some people make comments on the first page of an article rating its importance or usefulness, such as "Just background stuff," or "Best I've read yet!" Remember, you can always change your mind. Eventually, you will record on your articles and notes the Roman Numeral of the section in your paper where you will use specific information.

READING SOURCES AND TAKING NOTES . . .
OR, HOW AND WHY TO
SUMMARIZE, PARAPHRASE, AND DIRECTLY QUOTE

When people write research papers, they use information from many sources to support their opinion in order to convince a reader to agree. Writers need to achieve a balance in what they write and how they present it, or their paper becomes, well, BORING! Because sophisticated writers know this, they read their sources carefully and make decisions about how they will use each piece of information while they read.

When taking notes, experienced researchers do not simply copy word for word from their articles, books, pamphlets, broadcasts, interviews, or online sources, unless they plan to directly quote it. In the process of reading, they evaluate the importance and usefulness of what they learn, and they decide whether or not they think that it will be something they can use to support their opinion. This text does not teach the use note cards because they can get mixed up and get lost. Before there were copy machines, researchers spent hours in the libraries painstakingly taking notes on note cards, and placing the bibliographic information on each and every one—very tedious and repetitive. One of the easiest and quickest ways to read and evaluate sources is to highlight or underline important facts or statistics or opinions in each author's work. That is why it is so useful to make photocopies of each article. Certainly you know that you must not write in a library or other borrowed book or magazine. But you can write on your own copy in any fashion you like!

USING PHOTOCOPIES

Making copies of articles or sources you want to use in support of your opinion can be very beneficial. You can, in this way, get more out of your library time by being able to gather many more articles and sources while you are there, which you can then read, study and highlight with a marker at home, or in class. Many people find that using a three ring binder with dividers, and three hole punching (carefully--not through any print!) their copies, is a very secure and organized way to take care of their sources. As mentioned above, you can write and comment on your own copies to your heart's content. **JUST A WORD TO THE WISE, HOWEVER; BEFORE YOU PUT AWAY A SOURCE YOU HAVE PHOTOCOPIED, MAKE SURE YOU RECORD ALL THE NECESSARY BIBLIOGRAPHIC INFORMATION ABOUT IT ON THE COPY ITSELF, AND ON YOUR WORKING BIBLIOGRAPHY.**

Libraries charge 10 to 15 cents per copy; to save money some people check out magazines and copy them more cheaply elsewhere. Most students think the cost is well worth it because they can gather and manage, study and safely transport so much more research material this way. A word to the wise: copying an article you have sent to yourself by email is more expensive than using the library copier. Be economical!

WHAT'S THE NEXT STEP AFTER HIGHLIGHTING
AND WRITING NOTES ON PHOTOCOPIES?

In general, you can transfer source material into your notes or preliminary outline or onto note cards in three different ways: you can summarize, or you can paraphrase, or you can directly quote. A summary reports the main points of an article. It is used to shorten an author's work considerably. A paraphrase is almost like a translation—practically a word for word interpretation—from what some people call "hard" English to "easy" English. It is used to change technical language into the everyday language people use. Direct quotes are used when you determine that the author said it so well, it should not be shortened, or it doesn't need translation. What follows is an explanation of these three methods. **Each has a specific use.**

WRITING A SUMMARY

Use a summary when you want to give the main points from a long piece of information. A summary, also called a precis, is a brief restatement in your own words of the main ideas of a passage, article, or an entire book.

First, begin your summary with an introduction that explains where the information is coming from; for instance, mention the author's name and/or the title of the article. You can also briefly explain why it is significant to your opinion.

This introduces information

In a *Newsweek* article by Gray entitled "Leap of Faith," the extent of documented abuse of gymnasts is appalling. Almost no gymnast participates in the sport without suffering an injury that requires more attention than a bruise or scrape does. A study in the *New England Journal of Medicine* states that there is abundant evidence of long-term physical damage experienced by female gymnasts. It concluded that there are large numbers of injuries from overtraining, which supports the allegation that gymnasts are physically abused (271). This *shows the significance to the writer's thesis.*

Second, a summary must present all those main ideas <u>in the exact same order</u> as the author wrote them. [In most persuasive writing, authors save their best, most convincing information, reason, or example to present last because people remember best what they heard or read last. So <u>authors save the best for last</u>. Remember that principle in your own writing!] If you change the order of the author's points, then, you have changed the author's intent and meaning. That's not fair to the author, so don't do it; don't change the order or leave any main point out.

This is chronological order. It shows how Christy's problem progressed to desperation.

One example of the heartbreak a judge can cause is shown with this history of a former gymnast. At a meet, one of America's many sweethearts, Christy Henrich, was told by a judge that if she lost weight, she might have a shot at the Olympics. When Christy heard this, she decided that the only way she would be worth anything as a person was if she lost weight (and thus became an Olympian). She lost weight by doing nonstop exercise, thus developing anorexia and bulimia. At one point in her life, she was so desperate to lose weight that she asked Bo Moreno, a wrestler, how members of the wrestling team lost weight. He told her they wore plastic, ran with the steam on in the shower, and they took Ex Lax. What he didn't know was that Christy had already tried every one of those strategies (Blandford 73).

Third, omit the examples, asides, and analogies (comparisons) that authors use to illustrate their points and to interest their readers. Like Sgt. Friday, you just want to "stick to the facts, Ma'am."

Since the idea of the perfect female body has changed so drastically in the last several decades, the girls feel media pressure to look like the "perfect" woman (Noden 54). With the changing ideal of the perfect body, the standard for gymnasts' bodies has changed as well. The image of the world-class gymnast as waif has only become more exaggerated in the (last) three decades... the average size of the women on the U.S. Olympic team has shrunk from 5'3", 105 pounds in 1976, to 4'9", 88 pounds in 2004" (58). In the past 30 years, gymnasts have become much smaller (58). To summarize, delete the specific details from "three decades—88 pounds in 2004."

Fourth, remain faithful to the meaning and spirit of the original. Do not take something out of context which an author wrote, to improperly make it seem that the author supports something you believe. That is unfair and unethical.

Fifth, do not change the author's tone about the subject. If an author is serious in his/her attitude, your report of it should be, too.

> Media coverage puts quite a bit of stress on the gymnasts as well. An example of this is shown in Christy Henrich's case. Christy was a world class gymnast. Bo Moreno, Henrich's fiancé, alleged that our country destroyed Christy Henrich through pressure from the media, and that therefore, we are to blame for her death. Bo read this {sappy} poem at her funeral: ***DO NOT EDITORIALIZE OR SHOW THE BIAS OF YOUR OPINION IN YOUR SUMMARY OF A SOURCE—**delete sappy.*
>
> "America's sweetheart brought to her knees, Willing to do anything to please, A product of our country, Pushed too far . . ." (Noden 54).

Sixth, your summary should not include any of your own ideas or observations.

An additional concern about gymnastics is the social isolation or social abuse. Once a gymnast becomes a woman, her career dissipates, and when the sport is no longer in her life, she does not know what to do. She has lived in the gym for so long that she is not used to socializing with people in her schools and community. She has traded more than a childhood for a shot at glory. She has traded basic social skills as well (Ryan 7). {So it is really not entirely a gymnast's fault is she is a spoiled brat and a social misfit; Ryan would like us to believe that that's the way she was brought up.} ***AGAIN, DO NOT GIVE YOUR OPINION OF A SOURCE WITHIN YOUR SUMMARY.*** *There is a place for it after the summary, or in your conclusion.*

Finally, a summary is approximately one-fourth to one-third the length of the original's length.

Here's how to write a summary:

As you read an article, **you will be looking for the main and important ideas.** They frequently are **the topic sentence** of a paragraph. Don't be fooled: the topic sentence is not necessarily always the first sentence of a paragraph. So look for the point or opinion that all the other sentences and ideas support; when you find it, it is the topic sentence. <u>Underline</u> or highlight it. **Look also for headings or key words**, or **new words** and their definitions. Mark **statistics** and **quotes** that back up your opinion.

After you have finished reading and marking your copy, **go back to the beginning. Decide which things you have underlined or highlighted are <u>main points</u>** and which things are evidence to support them. **NUMBER THE MAIN IDEAS IN YOUR MARGIN.** Now you will be able to write them in your own words and organize them in the correct order into a summary.

After you have written your summary, double check to make sure that it conveys the meaning and tone of the original in the main points and their order. Check that you have not missed anything or included your own ideas. You can use some words from the source, of course. As a rule, you can use the same names and technical terms. Have you condensed the material enough without omitting something important? Is it written clearly? Before you put it aside, BE SURE YOU ALSO INCLUDE THE PARENTHETICAL DOCUMENTATION so that you don't have to use valuable time looking it up again. You need the author's name and the exact page number(s) where the ideas were in the original. Write both in parentheses after your summary.

WRITING A PARAPHRASE

Paraphrasing is essentially translating an author's language into your own. You are to capture a fairly complete sense of an author's ideas without using the author's words. For this reason, paraphrase is especially useful for explaining technical material to a general audience. Paraphrase is also useful for conveying the essence of dialogue or for reporting complex material into easily understood terms. Moreover, the very act of putting someone else's ideas into your own words helps you to gain a better understanding of what has been written. It is therefore a good idea to develop your skill in this area by paraphrasing important material as soon as you finish reading it. It is a super study skill for a subject that is completely new to you, or that is truly complex. Have a dictionary and a thesaurus at hand, and use them!

PARAPHRASING IS A TOOL AND SKILL USEFUL FOR AT LEAST TWO PURPOSES:

1.   To clarify for the reader what he/she is reading, and

2.   To take notes for possible use in a research paper and/or for study. (NOTE: Whether an exact quotation or a paraphrase or a summary is used, credit must be given to the source with the use of PARENTHETICAL DOCUMENTATION; otherwise, the material used is *plagiarized.*)

PARAPHRASE has four qualifications:

1.   It must preserve the source's meaning.

2. It must preserve the source's viewpoint and tone.

3. It must not be so similar to the original in words or construction that it plagiarizes.

4. It is similar in length to the original.

To paraphrase, then:
First, introduce the source of the paraphrase.

Second, indicate an author's main points, and the minor points and statistics used to explain or illustrate them.

Third, be sure to follow the author's order and emphasis.

Fourth, quote brief phrases from the original to convey its tone or viewpoint, or if there is simply no other way to say it!

Fifth, a paraphrase is often the same length as the original; sometimes it can even be longer.

After you have written your paraphrase, make certain that you have avoided the phrasing of the original or quoted it, and that you have put double quotation marks around technical terms taken from your source. Make sure you have included all the important points. Insert any transitional words or phrases that are needed to make your paraphrase flow smoothly. **BE SURE YOU ALSO INCLUDE THE PARENTHETICAL DOCUMENTATION** at the end of the paraphrase so you do not have to waste time going back to look for it.

WRITING WITH DIRECT QUOTATIONS

Directly quoting an author is usually not a problem. It means that you will record word for word what the author said or wrote. If the author has made a spelling or grammar error, DO NOT CORRECT IT, because then you have changed the quote. Instead, after the mistake, write in parentheses the Latin word "sic." It means "thus" or "so," and readers will know that you did not make an error; you reported the quotation as it was written. For example: "Lee Harvey Oswald shot President Kenedy" (sic). If you have to add something or explain something in your own words within a direct quote, or add words to make the sentence of your text grammatically correct, place it inside square brackets [ ]. If your computer or typewriter does not have that key, write them in by hand.

For the clarity and flow of your writing, you should introduce a quote. There are several ways you can accomplish this: by stating the author's name; by referring to the title of the article; by explaining why this quote is important; by explaining how it is connected to the idea that precedes or follows it.

The other rules about using a direct quote are both related to the quote's length. Short quotes up to four lines are incorporated into your text. Quotations longer than four lines are indented 10 spaces from the left hand margin. This is explained in detail in the section on Parenthetical Documentation.

SUMMARY AND PARAPHRASE: A COMPARISON AND CONTRAST

SUMMARY does what paraphrase does, but it condenses the original so that the summary is one-fourth to one-third as long. Thus, it must omit details while retaining the main points. It may make use of some direct quotations, but only when necessary to preserve the tone of the original or when there are no true substitutes for certain words. **YOU MUST USE PARENTHETICAL DOCUMENTATION.**

SUMMARY EXERCISE

Now that you've learned what a summary is and how to do one, it is time to practice writing a summary and discuss the method and resulting paragraphs. Once you know you have been successful, you can go on to do the paraphrase exercise. When you have been equally as successful with that, then you know you are ready to go on to reading and summarizing, paraphrasing, and taking notes on your own articles.

The following advice by the highly respected news columnist Ann Landers appeared in the *Journal Times* [Racine, Wisconsin], dated Wednesday, January 1, 1986. It was entitled "ANN OFFERS TIPS FOR THE NEW YEAR."

DIRECTIONS: As you read the following column, number the five main ideas Ann Landers has for making the new year better. First, underline the topic sentences that represent those five ideas; then number them in order. Whoops! Here's a challenge for you—one of the ideas is not stated in a topic sentence; instead it is implied. When you find this bad habit (at which Ann hints by using sarcasm), mark it with an X and write what it is in your own words, in addition to giving it a number. Next, be careful; part of Ann's letter is a narrative description of a personal experience. It isn't a main idea—it is an illustration of one. Circle that section to keep from using any of it as a main idea. At the end of the letter, write a summary of five to seven sentences in your own words, on loose-leaf paper.

Dear Readers:

Are you reading this column through bloodshot eyes? Does the bottom of your mouth taste like the bottom of a birdcage? Did you make a fool of yourself last night? Or don't you remember? Well—anyway . . . HAPP----EEE NEW YEAR!

Sorry about your headache. Are you up to reading on? If not, crawl back into the sack and meet me here at this same place tomorrow.

For those of you who are still with me, I have a few suggestions that might make this new year a better one than last. First--if you are a smoker, quit. You'll feel better, look better, smell better, like yourself better and add years to your life. Your family will be thrilled, and people won't move away from you at cocktail parties, business meetings and dinners.

Have you been wanting to lose 20 pounds, or 30 or 40? Make this the year it happens. Only you are responsible for what goes into your mouth. If you have decided that diets don't work, you have come to terms with one of life's verities: DIETS DON'T WORK. Just look at the people who have tried every diet that comes down the pike. They're still fat. They've taken off a thousand pounds. Fifty off and fifty on—30 off and 40 on. These people are better off to stay fat. Yo-yoing is bad for the heart. The only sensible way to lose weight and keep it off is to change your eating habits. It's called behavior modification. I learned several years ago that my Waterloo was going to the refrigerator AFTER dinner.

I'd sit down to the typewriter after finishing a good meal (with dessert) and in half an hour I was back in the kitchen looking for a sliver of that great chocolate pie. Of course, a sliver was never enough. In 20 minutes I was back again for another sliver, only this time it was more like a wedge. A half hour later I made a return trip to the kitchen and ran into the almonds. I remembered that nuts are nutritious—rich in protein. So I took a handful. One helping of almonds is never enough, so, of course, I went back for a second.

After dinner I put away almost as many calories as I did at the table.

What saved me was 50 minutes of exercise every morning and the fact that I walked every place I could. But I knew I couldn't keep that up forever because when the years roll by the metabolism changes. It gets harder and harder--so I decided I had to cut out those nightly treks to the fridge. This one change in behavior has kept my weight stable for years.

I can't say enough about the value of exercise. It's good for the heart, the blood pressure, digestion, complexion and skin tone, and it generates energy.

Make a few resolutions about how you are going to treat the people around you. It's strange how often we treat those who are nearest and dearest the worst. We are courteous to strangers, casual friends and bosses, but we tend to be rude, short-tempered and inconsiderate to those we love best. How about making a resolution to be especially kind to wives, husbands, in-laws, children, sisters, brothers and parents? They will react with surprise and pleasure, and they are bound to be enormously grateful. Good will, kindness and thoughtfulness are like a boomerang. They always come back to you. Cast your bread upon the waters and you will get back sandwiches. Trust me.

YOUR SUMMARY:

_____

_____

_____

_____

_____

_____

_____

_____

PARAPHRASE EXERCISE

DIRECTIONS: Immediately below each of the following sentences, paraphrase the words which are underlined with words of your own. You may use a dictionary or thesaurus. You may change words and phrases that are not underlined as long as you do not change their meaning, but you should write clear and grammatically correct sentences.

1. In the <u>overwhelming majority of instances</u>, feelings of depression are not <u>indicative</u> of any <u>true disorder.</u>

2. Problems arise, however, when the depression becomes so <u>severe</u> or <u>prolonged</u> as to <u>produce a noticeable change</u> in a person's <u>lifestyle and behavior.</u>

3. "Exogenous" depressions are those in which an individual <u>reacts inordinately to some precipitating situation,</u> such as the death of a loved one or a major business failure.

4. Such reactions may be <u>prolonged and incapacitating.</u>

5. Other persons seem to have been depressed <u>all of their lives,</u> and their <u>self-esteem</u> is <u>chronically rock bottom.</u>

6. Finally, "endogenous" depressions have a <u>definite onset,</u> but no <u>external precipitating factor</u> can be <u>identified.</u>

7. Such depressions, which <u>occur more frequently</u> among the elderly, are characterized by <u>marked apathy and decreased appetite.</u>

(PARENTHETICAL DOCUMENTATION)

You have now spent a lot of time in the libraries, collecting information on sources, recording it on your Working Bibliography, and then finding the actual magazine articles. Hopefully, you will be able to make photocopies of the articles; library time is better spent collecting many articles than in writing notes on one or two. Some reference materials cannot be taken out of the library, and so photocopy those as well, or take good notes. The more you photocopy, the better. If you have the copies to take home with you, you can use a three hole punch and put them in a loose-leaf binder, using dividers to organize them by subtopic. In any case, if you have the copies, you can study and read them anytime that is convenient to you, and you can mark them as well, with highlighters or pen.

After you learn how to document your sources parenthetically with the information you collected for your Works Cited, you will be able to do a thorough job of taking notes.

WHAT TO DOCUMENT

Parenthetically document? That's a mouthful! More importantly, what does it mean? In writing your research paper, you must document, that is, explain the source for everything you put in your paper from your magazine articles, books, online information--all of it. You must document direct quotations. You also must document summaries you've written of an author's ideas. After all, YOU did not think them up, even if you put the ideas in your own words. The same goes for paraphrasing--just because you change an author's vocabulary doesn't mean that the idea started in your brain. Of course, common sense as well as ethics (knowing right from wrong) should determine what you document. For example, you rarely need to give sources for familiar proverbs (You can't judge a book by its cover), well-known quotations (We Shall Overcome), or common knowledge (George Washington was the first President of the United States). But you MUST indicate the source of any appropriated material that your readers might otherwise think you created.

The list of Works Cited at the end of your research paper plays an important role in your acknowledgment of sources, but *it does not in itself provide sufficiently detailed and precise documentation*. If you just have that list at the end of your paper, how will your readers know who said what in your paper? So, each time you write something in your paper from one of your articles or books, etc., you must indicate its exact source. People used to do this by making foot notes, numbered notes at the bottom of each page that corresponded to numbers next to ideas in the text. You probably have textbooks that use foot notes, probably with new vocabulary words. That is a really old-fashioned way of documenting, and various organizations have come up with easier methods. This textbook relies on the rules set up in the 7th edition of the *MLA Handbook for Writers of Research Papers*, which is published by the National Council of Teachers of English. MLA stands for Modern Language Association.

The most practical way to supply this information is to insert brief **parenthetical acknowledgments** in your paper wherever you incorporate another's words, facts, or ideas. <u>Usually the author's last name and a page number within parentheses</u> (hence the name parenthetical documentation) are enough to identify the source and the specific location from which you have borrowed material. Thus, the full information about where that information came from is later supplied in the Works Cited. For every quote, summary or paraphrase of someone else's work, you must include the name of the source and the exact page number where you found it, right after you write it, AND you must have the corresponding complete publication information in your Works Cited.

YOU MAY NOT HAVE ANY DOCUMENTATION IN THE TEXT OF YOUR PAPER THAT IS NOT KEYED TO AN ENTRY ON THE WORKS CITED!

You certainly won't be shocked to know that there are certain rules to follow when writing your parenthetical documentation, but there aren't too many, and after the rules are listed below, you will find a sample page of a paper which illustrates them.

PARENTHETICAL REFERENCE STYLES

A work with one author: If the work has only one author, enclose the author's last name and the page number(s) of the exact page location in parentheses. If there is no page, type in n.p. for no page. Do not use the word "page" or its abbreviation "p." or "pp." anywhere in the parenthetical documentation. No p'ing in the paper! Example: (LoCurto 40).

If you state the author's name in the text, you need only cite the page if no other author's work comes in between. Ex.: (40)

A work with two authors: If a work has two authors, give the last name of each person listed, IN THE SAME ORDER AS ON THE TITLE PAGE OF THE BOOK OR ARTICLE (don't alphabetize these!) tying them together with the word "and," and give the page reference. Again, no punctuation inside the parentheses. Example: (Hayes and Strausser 51).

A work with three authors: Type the three last names with a comma and a space after the first and second names, then the word "and," space, and the third last name. Example:

(Fong, Stafford, and Runge 44). Again, if you cite the authors' names in the text, you need only cite the page, as above. (44)

A work with four or more authors: Type in parentheses the first author's last name, space, and the Latin words "et al," which mean "and more." Example: (Fredrick et al 31). Again, if the authors' names appear in the text, you need only cite the page (31).

Author of several works used in research: If you use more than one article, text, or such by a single author in your research paper, include in parentheses the author's last name, a comma, a space, and the title of the work, if brief; otherwise you may shorten it to the first three words, add an ellipsis (. . .), and enclose it in double quotation marks if it is an article, or underline or italicize it if it is a book. Then type one space and then the page number(s). Example: (Twain, *Tom Sawyer* 47)

Two authors with the same last name: If you have two authors with the same last name, you must use the author's first name's initial to differentiate it from the other. Then follow it with a period, a space, and then the last name. If the initial is the same for both authors, you must type in the whole first name.

Example: (M. Lopez 52) and (D. Lopez 14)

No author given for an article: If the quote or statistic or summary or paraphrase is taken from an article or book without an author or editor, use just the title of the article (in quotation marks) or book (underlined) and the page number(s) in the parenthetical reference. Example: ("Faraway Places" 79)

PUNCTUATION RULES FOR PERIODS AND COMMAS WITH PARENTHETICAL DOCUMENTATION

There are just two rules: The **After Rule** and the **Before Rule**.

The AFTER RULE:

The period or comma is **ALWAYS** placed immediately **AFTER** the parenthetical documentation for: 1. a short (four lines or less) quotation; 2. any summary, or 3. Any paraphrase. Note the use of only one space between the double quotation marks of the quotation and the parenthesis. For example:

"While shark attacks do occur, riding to the beach in a car remains far more

hazardous than swimming once you get there" (Gray 6).

The BEFORE RULE:

With a LONG quotation (**ONLY**) that takes more than four typed lines, it is necessary to indent the entire quotation by ten typed spaces or two inches if handwritten, from the left hand margin ONLY. (Do not change the one inch margin on the right side of the paper.)

In such a case, at the end of a long, set off quotation, the period and two spaces are placed **BEFORE** the parenthetical documentation. Also, because the quotation is being set off with the double indentation, everyone who reads the paper will recognize that it is a direct quote. Therefore, NO QUOTATION MARKS ARE USED WHATSOEVER because it would be redundant. An example follows.

The First World War brought about new financial problems for people who wanted

loans. The Federal government required assurance that any borrowed funds would be repaid, so people had to find different ways to finance their mortgage and loan needs. Financing the war was very difficult at the time.

> Baring Brothers, a banking firm for the enemy country, handled routine accounts for the United States overseas, but the firm would take on no new loans. Funding was extremely difficult to obtain, which is one of the reasons credit unions began to flourish. Many organizations and companies created their own credit unions. A great example of the use of credit unions is seen in the movie favorite, *It's a Wonderful Life.* (Rodriguez 325)

Sometimes in using a direct quotation, you may not want to include everything, but just certain parts. There is a way to do that comfortably as long as you keep two principles in mind. You must be fair to the author and not quote something out of context, or in any way twist what he or she really meant. The second principle is that you must keep your writing and that of the quotation grammatically correct as you go from one idea to the other.

When you quote only a word or two from an author, the words will appear in quotation marks in your writing. But if you want to quote only certain parts of something longer, you will use an **ellipsis** to show where words from the quotation are missing. An **ellipsis** consists of three spaced periods, that is, three periods with a space before each, and one space after the last period (. . .). Here is an example:

> Shuman explains that gifted students placed in an interdisciplinary curriculum can see "the interrelationships and interdependence of knowledge . . ." better than if they were in single courses showing no relationship or application to others (49).

If you decide to end your quotation with an ellipsis, type your three spaced periods as above, type your parenthetical documentation, and then add the final period. Here is another example:

> "One of the delights of working with academically gifted young people is their ability to make connections. They discover analogies, parallels, contrasts, and contradictions . . . they interrelate and associate concepts and observe diverse and unusual relationships . . ." (Baumann and Meyer 48). The authors go on to explain other connections.

If you use a long, indented quotation that ends with an ellipsis, type the last word, immediately type a period, then space period space period space period. Follow with two spaces and then your parenthetical documentation. For example:

A primary theme of the novel by John Steinbeck, *The Pearl*, can be illustrated by one of the Biblical parables which concludes with this passage:

> Lay not up for yourselves treasures upon earth, where moth and rust doth corrupt, and where thieves break through and steal: But lay up for yourselves treasures in heaven, where neither moth nor rust doth corrupt, and where thieves do not break through nor steal: For where your treasure is, there will your heart be also. . . . (*Revised Standard Bible*, Matthew 6: 19-21)

THE THESIS SENTENCE

The THESIS SENTENCE of a research paper is the most important sentence in the paper. It is the statement around which the entire paper revolves. The THESIS SENTENCE expresses your knowledgeable opinion about a subject. Everything in the paper is in some way supportive of that statement. **THE THESIS SENTENCE IS THE FOCUS OF YOUR ENTIRE RESEARCH PAPER.** Everything in your paper is in some way supportive of that thesis sentence; each paragraph you write will supply information, examples, explanations, definitions, statistics, reasons or proof that your thesis sentence is correct.

These are the things you need to know to write a thesis sentence:

1. The two purposes of the thesis sentence are:

    A. To act as a guide for the writer to stay focused on his/her job

    B. To act as a contract between the writer and the reader. In essence, the writer presents a statement of opinion in such a way that it seems like a fact, with the expectation or promise that following evidence will clearly prove it.

2. The thesis sentence should do these three things:

    A. Express your opinion

    B. Be direct, straightforward and clear

    C. Be concise; be brief.

3. Word choice is critical, not only in the meaning it presents, but in the grammatical way in which it is structured. You want your choice of words to gain the reader's attention immediately, create an interest in your subject and opinion, and be crystal clear.

4. The way you write your thesis sentence is crucial; it can make or break your research paper. You need to construct it carefully to express your opinion positively, assertively, and clearly. **Never refer to the word I, or use the words "in my opinion," or "in this report," or "in this paper."** They weaken your credibility. First of all, the reader knows you are expressing your opinion. Secondly, your reader knows he or she is reading a paper! Get on with it.

5. This is a hard principle to accept, but it is part of writing research papers: Remember that your purpose is to be successfully persuasive. If you read all your sources and find that they actually oppose your opinion, FOR THE PURPOSE OF A SCHOOL ASSIGNMENT which has the goal of earning a good grade, you should decide to write the paper from the point of view which has the most support from the research you have done, even if you disagree with it in your heart. That is why it is important to choose your topic carefully. You should choose a topic that is controversial so that there is room for argument, but not one that you will logically lose.

SAMPLE THESIS SENTENCES AND THEIR CORRECTIONS

The best way to learn to write good thesis sentences is to just dive in and try. First, write three different sentences for your topic.

1._____

2._____

3._____

Now, with a group of two or three other students, read and discuss them. Vote on each person's best sentence. Make improvements collaboratively if you can. The next thing to do as a whole class is discuss, and correct a lot of sentences; your classmates' sentences are the best to use because you will all learn from and with each other as you read, listen, think, evaluate, and make suggestions on how to make each sentence better. Keep track of all the sentences by writing down the first attempts, and then recording the class's new and improved versions. Keep this list of sentences in your binder to refer to the next time you write a research paper--it will help you formulate a good thesis sentence.

Here is a sample of, quite frankly, a lousy thesis sentence by a favorite and superior student of mine (student leader, athlete and musician as well!) named Joe Medendorp. Joe gave me permission to use this sentence in all my classes because we all learned so much from critiquing and improving it. His topic was Genetic Research. Here is his sentence:

Genetics, after all, is very controversial, but I still firmly believe that we should go ahead with technology.

What do you think about this sentence? Is it clear--do you really know what he wants us to think? Is it assertive and strong? Is it brief and to the point? The answer to those the last three questions is undeniably "No." Here is what is wrong.

    [delays]   [weakens your position]   [no I!]   [again weakens and whines]   [too vague]
Genetics, after all, is very controversial, but I still firmly believe that we should go ahead
[too vague]   [too long!]
with technology.

We asked Joe what he really wanted to say. At first it was hard for him to put it into words; he was kind of stuck on his first sentence, and just didn't know how to fix it. We asked him, "Joe, who do you mean by 'we'?" And he said, "The United States." Then we asked him what he meant by technology, and he said, "Genetics engineering." We asked him what he meant by "go ahead" with it, and he said that he thought the government should support research in genetic engineering. Then we asked him why he thought so, and he replied, "Because genetics engineering can make human beings overcome disease and hereditary birth defects." Then we asked Joe why he didn't just say that, and we all laughed, Joe included. Here is the sentence we put together with Joe, based on the questions we asked him.

The U.S. should promote genetics research to enhance human life.

Isn't that MUCH better?

Try to write your thesis sentence in different ways here:

_____

_____

_____

_____

_____

_____

_____

_____

THE FUNCTIONAL INTRODUCTION SENTENCE(S)

First, don't let the names confuse you. The introductory paragraph to your paper is not the same thing as the Functional Introduction sentence(s). The Functional Introduction sentence(s) are part of your entire introduction.

The FUNCTIONAL INTRODUCTION is one or two or three sentences found in your introductory paragraph, usually after your thesis sentence. The Functional Introduction sentence(s) are to a writer and a reader what a blueprint is to an architect. These sentences are a mini-outline of the rest of your paper. They lay out the major points or subtopics you will use to prove your thesis in an order which you will carefully and logically decide. Your paper's entire structure must follow in exactly the same order as the Functional Introduction states them. This sophisticated technique of writing is called Parallel Structure.

Parallel Structure is important to the organization of your paper. Once you have decided your knowledgeable opinion and have constructed a great thesis sentence, you should also have figured out the best way to present all your supporting information in order to persuade your reader to agree with you. Thus the placement of each subtopic is in an order that you have decided is logical, and it also has meaning.

Remember when you read about Summarizing and Paraphrasing? It was important to keep authors' ideas in the exact same order as they presented them because there was meaning to the order. They may have felt one point was more important than the others, so they saved the best for last. You will do the same thing in your Functional Introduction and then in your paper.

Wouldn't it be confusing for a reader to read that you were going to prove your point with A, then B, then C, and then D, but then in your paper you present the information in the order D, B, A, C? The reader would wonder what you really had decided was the most important. By breaking the rule of Parallel Structure (your paper's structure is parallel to your Functional Introduction), you would, in a sense, be breaking your contract with the reader to be clear and logical. If you are not clear and logical, you won't be persuasive.

What happens if you decide as you write your paper that you like a different order for your subtopics than what you had earlier decided. Are you stuck with the first order? CERTAINLY NOT! Just go back and rewrite your Functional Introduction to reflect your new, revised order! What happens if you find new information that needs to go in the paper; can you use it? OF COURSE! Just be sure to go back and add it into your Functional Introduction.

How will you write your Functional Introduction?

Here's how:

1. Start by writing your thesis sentence at the top of a notebook page.

2. Draw several boxes, three to six, or more, if necessary.

3. In each box, write the name of the subtopic or the explanation of the kind of proof you have.

4. Then, number the boxes in the logical order you choose. The most logical pattern of organization is to go from the least important support to the most important support.

5. Write an outline of the introduction paragraph including hook, thesis and functional introduction.

6. Finally, write the sentence or sentences that express your Functional Introduction.

This was Alexis Gray's Thesis Sentence: Can you pick out the words that express her opinion? What words carry the topic?

The U.S. must relieve global hunger.

She drew six boxes with these subtopics, and then she organized them by number:

Why should the U.S. become involved? 4	What is global hunger? 1	What are the consequences of global hunger? 3
What are ways to relieve global hunger? 5	Why is there global hunger? 2	What are the benefits of curing global hunger? 6

Next she wrote an outline of the introduction , and then Alexis wrote her Functional Introduction in this way:

In order to relieve global hunger, we must know what it is and what causes it, and we must recognize its negative consequences. Then the U.S. must develop methods to relieve it in order that the world community will benefit.

Say you were to write a paper in which your thesis was "John F. Kennedy's assassination was the result of a conspiracy." Your research covered a lot of information, which you placed in the following order: what Kennedy had been like as a President so far, including his campaign for re-election; facts about the day of the assassination, information that negated the single bullet theory, and reasons people might have wanted him dead. In outline format, your Functional Introduction would be a list:

I.   Introduction Paragraph

    A.   Hook

    B.   Thesis

    C.   Functional Introduction

        1.   Kennedy's troubled Presidential History and campaign

        2.   The day of the Assassination

        3.   The single bullet theory

        4.   Conspiracy theories.

To turn the Functional Introduction outline into a sentence or two or three, you just tie the ideas all together. Each part of the Introductory Paragraph below is labeled. The Functional Introduction sentences are in bold print.

[---HOOK---------------------------
"The sounds of gunfire ripped through Dealey Plaza on that late November day in
---]

1963, and 30 minutes later, The President was dead" (Farmer 120). Who killed Kennedy?

[-----THESIS----------]   [FUNC. INTRO. #1--------

It wasn't just Lee Harvey Oswald; it was a conspiracy. **From the beginning of his**

----------]   [FUNC. INTRO.#2----

Presidency, JFK had made serious personal mistakes and faced critical national problems.
Witnesses of ---------------]   [FUNC. INTRO. #3-----

the assassination provided many troubling reports, and once the single bullet theory
------------------]   [FUNC. INTRO. #4-------------]

was proven incorrect, a number of conspiracy theories were presented. JFK was a
marked man.

THE INTRODUCTORY PARAGRAPH

As you have been reading and viewing your sources, you may have come across a real attention grabber, a heart stopper, a statement that made you stop and say, "Oh, Wow!" You undoubtedly marked those kinds of statements because they were so applicable to your thesis, you knew you would use them. Here is a new purpose for your reading and rereading: LOOK FOR THE "OH, WOW!" AND MARK IT. Why? Because you are going to need at least one "Oh, Wow!" to start your paper, and you may want to use an appropriate "Oh, Wow!" type statement in your Conclusion. Another name for the "Oh, Wow" is the **HOOK**. It is the statement that "hooks" your readers into wanting to continue reading your paper. It piques their curiosity and makes them want to be convinced. That is a great way to build the introduction to your persuasive research paper.

An Introduction prepares an audience for your paper. The preparation needed will depend on your subject, your audience, and your purpose. A strong introduction brings readers into the world of your paper, but a weak one leaves them outside. Not only must you bring readers into your paper through your introduction, you must also create interest. Your Introduction Paragraph(s) include your THESIS SENTENCE, your FUNCTIONAL INTRODUCTION and your HOOK, not necessarily in that order. Your introduction, usually a full paragraph of several sentences, and almost never a single sentence, and sometimes two or three paragraphs, must make clear to your audience what will follow.

Some introductions are straightforward, concerned primarily with presenting information. You can begin by announcing your subject, limiting it with the Thesis and then outlining the body with your Functional Introduction. Not all subjects appeal to all readers, and at times you must find a way to capture your audience's attention (HOOK). You might achieve this in one of the following ways:

Begin with a quotation from an established and recognized authority.

Begin by asking a question.

Begin with a definition of one of your important terms.

Begin by making a comparison or an analogy.

Begin with the significance (importance) of your thesis.

Begin with a narrative of someone's experience.

Begin with an example from the subject.

Begin with alarming or surprising statistics.

Begin with a list of problems to be solved.

RULES FOR OUTLINING:
HOW A FORMAL OUTLINE SHOULD LOOK

A Formal Outline is polished. It is strictly parallel and precise. The points made are presented in the exact order in which they will appear in the paper. Because your Research Paper's logic depends on it, a formal outline requires a lot of thought.

A Formal Outline indicates two things: the order in which you will present your ideas, and the relationship of the main ideas to supporting details. The outline format uses indentation and a specified system of symbols: Roman numerals, capital letters, Arabic numerals, and lower case letters, always with a period after each and followed by two spaces. This system indicates going from a general idea to a more specific one. Note: if a sentence must be carried to the next line, it must begin directly under the first letter of the sentence. Don't begin the second line flush with the margin. By following your indentations carefully, the white space surrounding symbols and headings makes the structure of your paper more clear.

1. Roman numerals indicate major divisions and are flush with the left margin of the page.

2. Capital letters precede division of secondary importance, and are indented slightly.

3. Arabic numerals, which signal major supporting examples, are indented further.

4. Lower case letters announce specific supporting details and are indented still further.

FOR EXAMPLE:
I. First Major division of your paper
    A.   First secondary division
        1.   First Supporting Detail
            a. First specific
            b. Second specific detail
        2.   Second Supporting detail
            a. First specific detail
            b. Second specific detail

    B.   Second secondary division
        1.
            a.
            b.
        2.
            a.
            b.
II. Second Major Division et cetera.................

Here's a question for you: After you have completed your Final Outline, can you change it before you write your Rough Draft if you find new information?

CERTAINLY!

You can change anything up until you turn in your final paper.

HOW TO HANDLE OPPOSING EVIDENCE

Precisely because you have chosen a controversial subject, you are likely to find information and evidence in your resources that oppose your viewpoint. You have to make three important decisions.

1. Is the information so powerful and overwhelming that you cannot overcome it with your other information? If it is, but you are not willing to change your mind in spite of it, perhaps you had better change your topic and start over. If that evidence is so damaging that the success of your persuasive thesis is in serious jeopardy, you will be fighting an uphill battle that you just cannot win. Sometimes this happens when you have chosen a topic that is based on religious, political or personal values.

2.   If, however, you are willing to be flexible and make a change, you can rewrite your thesis and functional introduction to reflect that, and still be able to make a successful paper. You may be surprised that you have learned something about yourself and your opinions. Sometimes they are not based on the facts.

    A student who planned to write a paper in favor of capital punishment discovered information on the number of teenagers on Death Row. Her research led her to discover alternatives for them including therapy and rehabilitation, and she ended up writing a paper which opposed capital punishment altogether!

3. Is the information damaging, but only in a minor way so that your thesis can still be successful? If so, you can still proceed.

First of all, you cannot simply ignore opposing (refuting) evidence. To do so would be unethical and unwise. Any reader who is aware of that evidence from another source would immediately discount your credibility (believability) because you attempted to ignore it and only presented one side of the issue.

The way to handle the information is to report it **without elaboration,** and **place it early in your paper.** Use transitional markers of concessions such as: **Although** so-and-so reported blah, blah, blah . . . it does not affect the overall outcome. Or **Even though** such-and-such happened, etc. Additional concession transitional markers are listed in the section entitled Transitions: Connecting Language, later in the book.

Remember the rule "What is read last, is remembered best, so save the best for last"? Don't bring up opposing information at the end of your paper. In a sense you "bury" it by placing it at the beginning and piling all your better, contradictory information on top of it. It works!

THE NEXT STEP: THE PRELIMINARY OUTLINE

Generally, people cannot read articles, highlight, underline and take notes on them, and then start writing their papers without a plan. Because of the length of the assignment--usually 8 to 12 pages-- writers need to take time to specifically outline their ideas before starting a rough draft. What follows is an explanation of how to do the Preliminary Outline, which is brief but includes the parenthetical documentation for each and every source. Later, you will learn how to do a Sentence Outline. The good news is that once you have done the Preliminary Outline, you will know exactly where you are going, and after you have written your Sentence Outline and have had it checked by your teacher, you will know that you have enough information, that it is logically organized, and it is correctly documented. Writing your rough draft of your paper will be a breeze after that.

HOW TO MAKE A PRELIMINARY OUTLINE

1.   After you have read a considerable amount (at least half) of your articles, books, pamphlets, etc., and you have written your thesis sentence, you should have been able to break down the evidence of your research resources into several (at least three) areas of information, also called subtopics, that will support your thesis sentence. This is what made up your Functional Introduction sentence(s).

In writing your Functional Introduction, you will have identified these subtopics, and put them into a specific, logical and persuasive order. That probably was from least to most important order, which is Persuasive Order. Within your subtopics you may also have developed ideas in a number of ways, such as;

   A.   Chronological (Time) Order;

   B.   Cause and Effect Relationship, (one cause → many effects; many causes →one effect; causal chain;

   C.   Comparison/Contrast (either by the Item-by-item Method, or by the Block Method);

   D.   Exemplification (giving examples);

   E.   Categorization; (analyze the parts that make up the whole) or

   F.   Definition.

2.   Whatever the order of your subtopics or the way in which you develop them, you should, for the sake of this Preliminary Outline, and the subsequent Sentence Outline, give each subtopic a Roman Numeral reflecting its order in the Functional Introduction. Your outline will start with Roman Numeral I. (always follow Roman Numerals and letters and numbers

with a period and at least two spaces) which will be your Introductory Paragraph. In your Introductory paragraph you will have three letters, A., B., and C., representing your HOOK, your THESIS, and your FUNCTIONAL INTRODUCTION. With your FUNCTIONAL INTRODUCTION, you will have at least three numbers representing your subtopics. Some people have many more than three, depending on the scope of their paper and the amount of information they have gathered. Your subsequent Roman Numerals will then list those subtopics mentioned in your Functional Introduction, in the same order.

Here is an example of the Preliminary Outline's Introduction:

I.   Introduction

      A.   Hook. Who killed President John F. Kennedy and why?

      B.   Thesis. JFK was assassinated as a result of a conspiracy.

      C.   Functional Introduction

            1.   JFK's controversial Presidential history and campaign

            2.   The day of the assassination

            3.   The single bullet theory

            4.   Conspiracy theories

3.   During the rest of your reading, highlighting, underlining and note-taking process, and as you reread your resources, READ WITH A NEW AND ADDITIONAL PURPOSE. Up until now you have read to learn and gain understanding of your topic's main issues, and to mark things you have evaluated for your use. NOW READ AND REREAD to fill in a Preliminary Outline and to look for possible HOOK material (you can always change it if you find something better) and for possible CONCLUSION material.

4.   Here's how to fill in a Preliminary Outline Rough Draft

Use one page of notebook paper for each of the subtopics of the body of your paper. Or, use different colored pieces of computer paper, thus color coding your major subtopics. It is more efficient because you can tell which subtopic is which more easily than looking for the Roman Numeral at the top. Label each page at the top with its Roman Numeral and its subtopic as listed in your Functional Introduction.

NOW, as you continue to read your articles and sources, decide which information you highlight in your resources belongs on which Preliminary Outline page (in which subtopic section). Record it there briefly, and include appropriate Parenthetical Documentation each and every time. You should not be surprised if you add a subtopic or two before you finish this process; if you do, be sure to add them to the Functional Introduction after you decide where they belong in the logical order you have planned.

See how each notebook page becomes the collection point for evidence you plan to use? You will have all your subtopic information in one place: on a piece of notebook or computer paper, which you can then organize for an outline by labeling each note with a capital letter, Arabic numeral, or lower case letter, depending on where it falls in your logical order. It is much less likely that you will lose notes this way than by using cards.

On each Preliminary Outline page, as you read and then write, record a short phrase, or the first several words from the information in the article you want to use as support for your opinion. RECORD THE NAME OF THE AUTHOR AND THE EXACT PAGE NUMBER FROM WITHIN THE ARTICLE/BOOK ETC., RIGHT NEXT TO IT IN PARENTHESES and Voila! You have your parenthetical documentation for that entry done! Be sure to carry forward this documentation when you place it in your Sentence Outline, Rough Draft, and Final Copy. If you forget to do this, you may have a hard time finding what you wanted to summarize, quote, or paraphrase, and you will have to search for the documentation all over again. BE SMART and EFFICIENT WITH YOUR PRECIOUS TIME. Remember, you must include this parenthetical documentation information each time you record information on your pages.

NEXT

Before you leave that resource and go onto another one, or even before you continue in that resource, take the time to WRITE IN THE TEXT OF THE ARTICLE THE ROMAN NUMERAL OF THE PRELIMINARY OUTLINE PAGE WHERE YOU HAVE RECORDED THE INFORMATION! Now you will know what information you want to use and where in your paper it will appear recorded in two different places: The articles themselves and the Preliminary Outline. Mark your text articles with S, P or DQ, for Summary, Paraphrase, or Direct Quote. Why not make this decision about how you will use information while you are thinking about it? Why do it again? This is just another back up, and really helpful when you go back to do the Sentence Outline and Rough Draft. It will make it so much easier to find the information you want to summarize, paraphrase, or directly quote.

Complete your Preliminary Outline by rereading all your sources until you are satisfied that you have all the information you need to make a successful persuasive research paper.

SAMPLE PAGES OF PRELIMINARY OUTLINE (rough draft)

Keep in mind that the information recorded on these pages was written *in the order in which the author looked at resources.* This order does not reflect any planning or logic yet; therefore, there are no capital letters in parts II through V, and there is no conclusion yet.

Notebook paper or colored page one	Notebook paper or colored page two

I. Introduction
 	
    A. Hook--sounds of gunfire (Flores 120)
 	
    B. Thesis--a conspiracy
    C. Functional Introduction
        1. Presidential History
        2. Assassination Day
        3. Single bullet theory
        4. Conspiracy theories
	II. Presidential History
	    Vietnam Opponents (Smith 27)
	
	    Cuban Missile Crisis (Jones 82-3)
	    Civil rights Movement (Arnold 73)
	    and (Egan 12)
	    Campaign Problems (Thomas 45-6)

Notebook paper or colored page three	Notebook paper or colored page four

III. Assassination Day
    Dealey Plaza
    (Thomas 43)
    Grassy Knoll   (Thomas 48)
    Security (Egan 184)
    Gov. Connally   (Syslack 18)
    Puff of Smoke
    (Dickert 121)
	IV. Single Bullet Theory
	    Types of Guns (Mrkvicka 66-7)
	
	    Trajectories (Dickert 122)
	    Physics (Benzow 22)
	    Connally? (Escobar 32)
	    Photographs (Zetina 16)

Notebook paper page five

V. Conspiracy Theories
    USSR Connection (Wilkinson 55-7)
 	
    Republican Party (Thomas 44)
    Cuban Retaliation (Jones 184)
    Mafia Opposition (Malke 233-4)
    Personal Morals (Syslack 55)

5.   Now reorganize all the citation sources recorded on each subtopic page into a logical, persuasive presentation of your support for your thesis. Use the formal outline format, including Roman Numerals, Subtopic Titles, Capital Letters, Arabic Numerals, and even lower case letters, if necessary. Mark this "sloppy copy" with the numbers and letters as you want them to appear in your final copy. **AGAIN, BE SURE YOU HAVE RECORDED THE NAME OF THE AUTHOR AND PAGE NUMBER FOR EACH CITATION YOU INCLUDE. Not only will it be required in the text of your paper as parenthetical documentation, but this information will provide you with all the citations you will need to acknowledge in your Works Cited list.**

SAMPLE PAGES OF FINAL PRELIMINARY OUTLINE PAGES

I. Introduction
    A. Hook
    B. Thesis--a conspiracy
    C. Functional Introduction
      1. Presidential History
      2. Assassination Day
      3. Single Bullet Theory
      4. Conspiracy Theories

II. Presidential History
    A. Cuban Missile Crisis (Jones 82-83)
    B. The Dirty Campaign (Adams 45)
    C. Vietnam War (Smith 27)
    D. Civil rights (Arnold 73: Egan 12)

III. Assassination Day
    A. Gov. Connally (Syslack 18)
    B. Dealey Plaza (Thomas 48)
    C. Security not Tight (Egan 184)
    D. Grassy Knoll (Thomas 48)
    E. Puff of Smoke (Dickert 121)

IV. Single Bullet Theory
    A. Photos (Morgan 16)
    B. Types of guns (Mrkvicka 66-7)
    C. Physics (Benzow 222)
    D. Trajectories (Dickert 122)
    E. War Protesters (Egan 26)

6. **When you have finished your Preliminary Outline, you will have done the hardest part of your paper, for you will have given your reading meaning by organizing a persuasive structure to support your Thesis.** You will have read, gained knowledge, evaluated and analyzed that knowledge, organized it and used it to prove a point. You will have demonstrated the use of the higher critical thinking skills. CONGRATULATIONS!

Maybe you should take a little break (a couple of days) while your teacher examines your outline and confers with you on changes and improvements

SAMPLE PRELIMINARY OUTLINE

Once you have reorganized your subtopics and the details within them, you will write or type up your Preliminary Outline starting on a new page and consolidating to save space. Here is a sample of Matt Tomkins' Preliminary Outline as he typed it up for a grade.

Jackie Robinson: A Hero for All Americans

I.   Introduction

    A.   Hook

        Jackie Robinson battled into an all white league. (Balos 11)

    B.   Thesis

        Jackie Robinson changed professional sports.

    C.   Functional Introduction

        1.   Athletic Talent

        2.   Recruitment

        3.   Battle for Racial Equality

        4.   Impact on American Society

II.   Jackie Robinson's Athletic Talent

    A.   Pre-Professional baseball accomplishments (Balos 3, 12)

    B.   Minor league statistics (Young 40)

    C.   First Year accomplishments (Balos 12)

    D.   He was a team leader (Murray 10)

    E.   Speed and fielding talent (Balos 12-13)

    F.   Career statistics (Young 42)

III.   Recruitment

       A.   Branch Rickey's plans (Young 36)

       B.   Scouting all over (Balos 3)

       C.   Robinson picked for ability and brains (Murray 10)

       D.   Meeting between Robinson and Rickey (Young 36-8)

Of course, the outline continues in the same manner. After the directions for writing a Sentence Outline, there will be a sample of Matt's Sentence Outline so that you can see how to progress from one to the next.

"LOVE IS A FALLACY" VOCABULARY

This vocabulary is used in the following essay which demonstrates fallacies of logic, which are ungrounded generalizations. You should avoid making these in your writing, and should not include them from your sources.   You must think about and evaluate the validity of your source material.

perspicacious -- having clear insight

acute -- perceptive

astute -- shrewd, clever

acme -- the highest point

Charleston -- a popular dance of the 1920's

cerebral -- marked by intellectual rather than passionate qualities

pin-up proportions -- sexually attractive girl whose picture boys like to hang in their locker

gamy -- the smell of spoiled game meat

Stutz Bearcat -- a sports car from around 1925

canny -- cautious, shrewd

waif -- a stray, helpless person, especially an abandoned or neglected child

resolutely – firmly; not turned from a purpose by difficulties or opposition or risk

waxing -- increasing

waning -- diminishing

bade -- bid

trysting -- meeting place of lovers

fallacy -- a piece of false reasoning

generalization -- a general rule or notion drawn or deduced from particular instances

contritely -- thoroughly sorry; sincerely apologetic

glumly -- gloomily

fraught -- filled with

analogy -- relationship between two things which are similar in many respects

pitchblende -- an ore from which uranium and radium are extracted

radium -- a shiny, white, metallic element, strongly radioactive, used in X-ray technology

Walter Pidgeon -- a famous leading man of the movies in the 1930's and 1940's

hypothesis -- an idea formed to provide the foundation of an argument

indignation -- anger aroused by injustice

hamstrung -- crippled

cretin -- a mentally retarded person

grueling -- exhausting

well-heeled -- quite wealthy (based on being able to afford many shoes!)

Pygmalion -- from Greek mythology: A Cypriot King and sculptor who fell in love with the statue he made and successfully begged Aphrodite to bring her to life

tolerant -- accepting

tactics -- carefully worked-out steps to achieve a goal

languish -- to become without vitality; to waste away

shambling -- awkward

reeled -- swayed unsteadily

Slang

nothing upstairs -- euphemism for not smart

Big Men on Campus -- the macho guys in the popular group

in the swim -- doing what the "in crowd" does

keen -- cool, nice

Holy Toledo! -- Oh, Wow! (Toledo, a capital of a province in Spain was the center of the Roman Catholic church, and there were seven cathedrals built on seven hills there.)

casual kick -- something for fun

delish -- delicious

marvy -- marvelous

sensaysh -- sensational

terrif -- terrific

magnif -- magnificent

knocked me out -- I loved it!

he fractured me -- I loved him!

pshaw -- phooey!

a knothead and a jitterbug -- a jerk

A HUMOROUS LOOK AT LOGIC

The following essay, written in 1951, is a great little lesson in logic taught with humor. A fallacy is something which is illogical; there is a fault in the line of reasoning. As you review your sources for content and their usefulness in your paper, have you ever questioned what an author was writing? Good! You shouldn't necessarily believe everything you read just because it has been published. Check the logic. If you can find a fallacy instead, you will avoid jumping to the wrong conclusion. There are eight fallacies presented in this essay. Your job is to identify them by name and example, and to be able to explain or define them.

See if you can figure out why this piece continues to be printed, many years after it was first published. Why might it not be written today? What is funny about this story? See if you can determine the meaning of the saying, "He was hoisted by his own petard."

Mostly, enjoy.

"Love is a Fallacy"
By Max Shulman

Cool was I and logical. Keen, calculating, perspicacious, acute, and astute--I was all of these. My brain was as powerful as a dynamo, as precise as a chemist's scales, as penetrating as a scalpel. And--think of it!--I was only eighteen.

It is not often that one so young has such a giant intellect. Take, for example, Petey Burch, my roommate at the University of Minnesota. Same age, same background, but dumb as an ox. A nice enough fellow, you understand, but nothing upstairs. Emotional type. Unstable. Impressionable. Worst of all, a faddist. Fads, I submit, are the very negation of reason. To be swept up in every new craze that comes along, to surrender yourself to idiocy just because everybody else is doing it--this, to me, is the acme of mindlessness. Not, however, to Petey.

One afternoon I found Petey lying on his bed with an expression of such distress on his face that I immediately diagnosed appendicitis. "Don't move," I said. "Don't take a laxative. I'll get a doctor."

"Raccoon," he mumbled thickly.

"Raccoon?" I said, pausing in my flight.

"I want a raccoon coat," he wailed.

I perceived that his trouble was not physical, but mental. "Why do you want a raccoon coat?"

"I should have known it," he cried, pounding his temples. "I should have known they'd come back when the Charleston came back. Like a fool I spent all my money for textbooks, and now I can't get a raccoon coat."

"Can you mean," I said incredulously, "that people are actually wearing raccoon coats again?"

"All the Big Men on Campus are wearing them. Where've you been?"

"In the library," I said, naming a place not frequented by Big Men on Campus.

He leaped from the bed and paced the room. "I've got to have a raccoon coat," he said passionately. "I've got to!"

"Petey, why? Look at it rationally. Raccoon coats are unsanitary. They shed. They smell bad. They weigh too much. They're unsightly. They--"

"You don't understand," he interrupted impatiently. "It's the thing to do. Don't you want to be in the swim?"

"No," I said truthfully.

"Well, I do," he declared. "I'd give anything for a raccoon coat. Anything!"

My brain, that precision instrument, slipped into high gear. "Anything?" I asked, looking at him narrowly.

"Anything," he affirmed in ringing tones.

I stroked my chin thoughtfully. It so happened that I knew where to get my hands on a raccoon coat. My father had had one in his undergraduate days; it lay now in a trunk in the attic back home. It also happened that Petey had something I wanted. He didn't have it exactly, but at least he had first rights on it. I refer to his girl, Polly Espy.

I had long coveted Polly Espy. Let me emphasize that my desire for this young woman was not emotional in nature. She was, to be sure, a girl who excited the emotions, but I was not one to let my heart rule my head. I wanted Polly for a shrewdly calculated, entirely cerebral reason.

I was a freshman in law school. In a few years I would be out in practice. I was well aware of the importance of the right kind of wife in furthering a lawyer's career. The successful lawyers I had observed were, almost without exception, married to beautiful, gracious, intelligent women. With one omission, Polly fitted these specifications perfectly.

Beautiful she was. She was not yet of pin-up proportions, but I felt sure that time would supply the lack. She already had the makings.

Gracious she was. By gracious I mean full of graces. She had an erectness of carriage, an ease of bearing, a poise that clearly indicated the best of breeding. At table her manners were exquisite. I had seen her at the Kozy Kampus Korner eating the specialty of the house--a sandwich that contained scraps of pot roast, gravy, chopped nuts, and a dipper of sauerkraut--without even getting her fingers moist.

Intelligent she was not. In fact, she veered in the opposite direction. But I believed that under my guidance she would smarten up. At any rate, it was worth a try. It is, after all, easier to make a beautiful dumb girl smart than to make an ugly smart girl beautiful.

"Petey," I said, "are you in love with Polly Espy?"

"I think she's a keen kid," he replied, "but I don't know if you'd call it love. Why?"

"Do you," I asked, "have any kind of formal arrangement with her? I mean are you going steady or anything like that?"

"No. We see each other quite a bit, but we both have other dates. Why?"

"Is there," I asked, "any other man for whom she has a particular fondness?"

"Not that I know of. Why?"

I nodded with satisfaction. "In other words, if you were out of the picture, the field would be open. Is that right?"

"I guess so. What are you getting at?"

"Nothing, nothing," I said innocently, and took my suitcase out of the closet.

"Where are you going?" asked Petey.

"Home for the weekend." I threw a few things into the bag.

"Listen," he said, clutching my arm eagerly, "while you're home, you couldn't get some money from your old man, could you, and lend it to me so I can buy a raccoon coat?"

"I may do better than that," I said with a mysterious wink and closed my bag and left.

~~~~~

"Look!" I said to Petey when I got back Monday morning. I threw open the suitcase and revealed the huge, hairy, gamy object that my father had worn in his Stutz Bearcat in 1925.

"Holy Toledo!" said Petey reverently. He plunged his hands into the raccoon coat and then his face. "Holy Toledo!" he repeated fifteen or twenty times.

"Would you like it?" I asked.

"Oh yes!" he cried, clutching the greasy pelt to him. Then a canny look came into his eyes. "What do you want for it?"

"Your girl," I said, mincing no words.

"Polly?" he said in a horrified whisper. "You want Polly?"

"That's right."

He flung the coat from him. "Never," he said stoutly.

I shrugged. "Okay. If you don't want to be in the swim, I guess it's your business."

I sat down in a chair and pretended to read a book, but out of the corner of my eye I kept watching Petey. He was a torn man. First, he looked at the coat with the expression of a waif at a bakery window. Then he turned away and set his jaw resolutely. Then he looked back at the coat, with even more longing in his face. Then he turned away, but with not so much resolution this time. Back and forth his head swiveled, desire waxing, resolution waning. Finally, he didn't turn away at all; he just stood and stared with mad lust at the coat.

"It isn't as though I was in love with Polly," he said thickly. "Or going steady or anything like that."

"That's right," I murmured.

"What's Polly to me, or me to Polly?"

"Not a thing," said I.

"It's just been a casual kick--just a few laughs, that's all."

"Try on the coat," said I.

He complied. The coat bunched high over his ears and dropped all the way down to his shoe tops. He looked like a mound of dead raccoons. "Fits fine," he said happily.

I rose from my chair. "Is it a deal?" I asked, extending my hand.

He swallowed. "It's a deal," he said and shook my hand.

~~~~~

I had my first date with Polly the following evening. This was in the nature of a survey; I wanted to find out just how much work I had to do to get her mind up to the standard I required. I took her first to dinner. "Gee, that was a delish dinner," she said as we left the restaurant. Then I took her to a movie. "Gee, that was a marvy movie," she said as we left the theater. And then I took her home. "Gee, I had a sensaysh time," she said as she bade me good night.

I went back to my room with a heavy heart. I had gravely underestimated the size of my task. This girl's lack of information was terrifying. Nor would it be enough merely to supply her with information. First she had to be taught to think. This loomed as a project of no small dimensions, and at first I was tempted to give her back to Petey. But then I got to thinking about her abundant physical charms and about the way she entered a room and the way she handled a knife and fork, and I decided to make an effort.

I went about it, as in all things, systematically. I gave her a course in logic. It happened that I, as a law student, was taking a course in logic myself, so I had all the facts at my finger tips. "Polly," I said to her when I picked her up on our next date, "tonight we are going over to the Knoll and talk."

"Oo, terrif," she replied. One thing I will say for this girl: You would go far to find another so agreeable.

We went to the Knoll, the campus trysting place, and we sat down under an old oak, and she looked at me expectantly. "What are we going to talk about?" she asked.

"Logic."

She thought this over for a minute and decided she liked it. "Magnif," she said.

"Logic," I said, clearing my throat, "is the science of thinking. Before we can think correctly, we must first learn to recognize the common fallacies of logic. These we will take up tonight."

"Wow-dow!" she cried, clapping her hands delightedly.

I winced, but went bravely on. "First let us examine the fallacy called Dicto Simpliciter."

"By all means," she urged, batting her lashes eagerly.

"Dicto Simpliciter means an argument based on an unqualified generalization. For example: Exercise is good. Therefore everybody should exercise."

"I agree," said Polly earnestly. "I mean exercise is wonderful. I mean it builds the body and everything."

"Polly," I said gently, "the argument is a fallacy. Exercise is good is an unqualified

generalization. For instance, if you have heart disease, exercise is bad, not good. Many people are ordered by their doctors not to exercise. You must qualify the generalization. You must say exercise is usually good, or exercise is good for most people. Otherwise you have committed a Dicto Simpliciter. Do you see?"

"No," she confessed. "But this is marvy. Do more! Do more!"

"It will be better if you stop tugging at my sleeve," I told her, and when she desisted, I continued. "Next we take up a fallacy called Hasty Generalization. Listen carefully: You can't speak French. I can't speak French. Petey Burch can't speak French. I must therefore conclude that nobody at the University of Minnesota can speak French."

"Really?" said Polly, amazed. "Nobody?"

I hid my exasperation. "Polly, it's a fallacy. The generalization is reached

too hastily. There are too few instances to support such a conclusion."

"Know any more fallacies?" she asked breathlessly. "This is more fun than dancing even."

I fought off a wave of despair. I was getting nowhere with this girl, absolutely nowhere. Still, I am nothing if not persistent. I continued. "Next comes Post Hoc. Listen to this: Let's not take Bill on our picnic. Every time we take him out with us, it rains.

"I know somebody just like that," she exclaimed. "A girl back home--Eula Becker, her name is. It never fails. Every single time we take her on a picnic--"

"Polly," I said sharply, "it's a fallacy. Eula Becker doesn't cause the rain. She has no connection with the rain. You are guilty of Post Hoc if you blame Eula Becker."

"I'll never do it again," she promised contritely. "Are you mad at me?"

I sighed deeply. "No, Polly, I'm not mad."

"Then tell me some more fallacies."

"All right. Let's try Contradictory Premises."

"Yes, let's," she chirped, blinking her eyes happily.

I frowned, but plunged ahead. "Here's an example of Contradictory Premises: If God can do anything, can He make a stone so heavy that He won't be able to lift it?"

"Of course," she replied promptly.

"But if He can do anything, He can lift the stone," I pointed out.

"Yeah," she said thoughtfully. "Well, then I guess He can't make the stone."

"But He can do anything," I reminded her.

She scratched her pretty, empty head. "I'm all confused," she admitted.

"Of course you are. Because when the premises of an argument contradict each other, there can be no argument. If there is an irresistible force, there can be no immovable object. If there is an immovable object, there can be no irresistible force. Get it?"

"Tell me some more of this keen stuff," she said eagerly.

I consulted my watch. "I think we'd better call it a night. I'll take you home now, and you go over all the things you've learned. We'll have another session tomorrow night."

I deposited her at the girls' dormitory, where she assured me that she had had a perfectly terrif evening, and I went glumly home to my room. Petey lay snoring in his bed, the raccoon coat huddled like a great hairy beast at his feet. For a moment I considered waking him and telling him that he could have his girl back. It seemed clear that my project was doomed to failure. The girl simply had a logic-proof head.

But then I reconsidered. I had wasted one evening; I might as well waste another. Who knew? Maybe somewhere in the extinct crater of her mind, a few embers still smoldered. Maybe somehow I could fan them into flame. Admittedly it was not a prospect fraught with hope, but I decided to give it one more try.

Seated under the oak the next evening, I said, "Our first fallacy tonight is called Ad Misericordiam."

She quivered with delight.

"Listen closely," I said. "A man applies for a job. When the boss asks him what his qualifications are, he replies that he has a wife and six children at home, the wife is a helpless cripple, the children have nothing to eat, no clothes to wear, no shoes on their feet, there are no beds in the house, no coal in the cellar, and winter is coming."

A tear rolled down each of Polly's pink cheeks. "Oh, this is awful, awful," she sobbed.

"Yes, it's awful," I agreed, "but it's no argument. The man never answered the boss's question about his qualifications. Instead he appealed to the boss's sympathy. He committed the fallacy of Ad Misericordiam. Do you understand?"

"Have you got a handkerchief?" she blubbered.

I handed her a handkerchief and tried to keep from screaming while she wiped her eyes. "Next," I said in a carefully controlled tone, "we will discuss False Analogy. Here is an example: Students should be allowed to look at their textbooks during examinations. After all, surgeons have X-rays to guide them during an operation, lawyers have briefs to guide them during a trial, and carpenters have blueprints to guide them when they are building a house. Why, then, shouldn't students be allowed to look at their textbooks during an examination?"

"There now," she said enthusiastically, "is the most marvy idea I've heard in years."

"Polly," I said testily, "the argument is all wrong. Doctors, lawyers, and carpenters aren't taking a test to see how much they have learned, but students are. The situations are altogether different, and you can't make an analogy between them."

"I still think it's a good idea," said Polly.

"Nuts," I muttered. Doggedly I pressed on. "Next we'll try Hypothesis Contrary to Fact."

"Sounds yummy," was Polly's reaction.

"Listen: If Madame Curie had not happened to leave a photographic plate in a drawer with a chunk of pitchblende, the world today would not know about radium."

"True, true," said Polly, nodding her head. "Did you see the movie? Oh, it just knocked me out. That Walter Pidgeon is so dreamy. I mean he fractures me."

"If you can forget Mr. Pidgeon for a moment," I said coldly, "I would like to point out that the statement is a fallacy. Maybe Madame Curie would have discovered radium at some later date. Maybe somebody else would have discovered it. Maybe any number of things would have happened. You can't start with a hypothesis that is not true and then draw any supportable conclusions from it."

"They ought to put Walter Pidgeon in more pictures," said Polly. "I hardly ever see him any more."

One more chance, I decided. But just one more. There is a limit to what flesh and blood can bear. "The next fallacy is called Poisoning the Well."

"How cute!" she gurgled.

"Two men are having a debate. The first one gets up and says, 'My opponent is a notorious liar. You can't believe a word that he is going to say.' . . . Now, Polly, think. Think hard. What's wrong?"

I watched her closely as she knit her creamy brow in concentration. Suddenly a glimmer of intelligence--the first I had seen--came into her eyes. "It's not fair," she said with indignation. "It's not a bit fair. What chance has the second man got if the first man calls him a liar before he even begins talking?"

"Right!" I cried exultantly. "One hundred per cent right. It's not fair. The first man has poisoned the well before anybody could drink from it. He has hamstrung his opponent before he could even start. . . . Polly, I'm proud of you."

"Pshaw," she murmured, blushing with pleasure.

"You see, my dear, these things aren't so hard. All you have to do is concentrate. Think--examine--evaluate. Come now, let's review everything we have learned."

"Fire away," she said with an airy wave of her hand.

Heartened by the knowledge that Polly was not altogether a cretin, I began a long, patient review of all I had told her. Over and over and over again I cited instances, pointed out flaws, kept hammering away without letup. It was like digging a tunnel. At first everything was work, sweat and darkness. I had no idea when I would reach the light, or even if I would. But I persisted. I pounded and clawed and scraped, and finally I was rewarded. I saw a chink of light. And then the chink got bigger and the sun came pouring in and all was bright.

Five grueling nights this took, but it was worth it. I had made a logician out of Polly; I had taught her to think. My job was done. She was worthy of me at last. She was a fit wife for me, a proper hostess for my many mansions, a suitable mother for my well-heeled children.

It must not be thought that I was without love for this girl. Quite the contrary. Just as Pygmalion loved the perfect woman he had fashioned, so I loved mine. I determined to acquaint her with my feelings at our very next meeting. The time had come to change our relationship from academic to romantic.

~~~~~

"Polly," I said when next we sat beneath our oak, "tonight we will not discuss fallacies."

"Aw, gee," she said, disappointed.

"My dear," I said, favoring her with a smile, "we have now spent five evenings together. We have gotten along splendidly. It is clear that we are well matched."

"Hasty Generalization," said Polly brightly.

"I beg your pardon," said I.

"Hasty Generalization," she repeated. "How can you say that we are well matched on the basis of only five dates?"

I chuckled with amusement. The dear child had learned her lessons well. "My dear," I said, patting her hand in a tolerant manner, "five dates is plenty. After all, you don't have to eat a whole cake to know that it's good."

"False Analogy," said Polly promptly. "I'm not a cake. I'm a girl."

I chuckled with somewhat less amusement. The dear child had learned her lessons perhaps too well. I decided to change tactics. Obviously the best approach was a simple, strong, direct declaration of love. I paused for a moment while my massive brain chose the proper words. Then I began:

"Polly, I love you. You are the whole world to me, and the moon and the stars and the constellations of outer space. Please, my darling, say that you will go steady with me, for if you will not, life will be meaningless. I will languish. I will refuse my meals. I will wander the face of the earth, a shambling, hollow-eyed hulk."

There, I thought, folding my arms, that ought to do it.

"Ad Misericordiam," said Polly.

I ground my teeth. I was not Pygmalion; I was Frankenstein, and my monster had me by the throat. Frantically I fought back the tide of panic surging through me. At all costs I had to keep cool.

"Well, Polly," I said, forcing a smile, "you certainly have learned your fallacies."

"You're darn right," she said with a vigorous nod.

"And who taught them to you, Polly?"

"You did."

"That's right. So you do owe me something, don't you dear? If I hadn't come along you never would have learned about fallacies."

"Hypothesis Contrary to Fact," she said instantly.

I dashed perspiration from my brow. "Polly," I croaked, "you mustn't take all these things so literally. I mean this is just classroom stuff. You know that the things you learn in school don't have anything to do with life."

"Dicto Simpliciter," she said, wagging her finger at me playfully.

That did it. I leaped to my feet, bellowing like a bull. "Will you or will you not go steady with me?"

"I will not," she replied.

"Why not?" I demanded.

"Because this afternoon I promised Petey Burch that I would go steady with him."

I reeled back, overcome with the infamy of it. After he promised, after he made a deal, after he shook my hand! "The rat!" I shrieked, kicking up great chunks of turf. "You can't go with him, Polly. He's a liar. He's a cheat. He's a rat."

"Poisoning the Well," said Polly, "and stop shouting. I think shouting must be a fallacy too."

With an immense effort of will, I modulated my voice. "All right," I said. "You're a logician. Let's look at this thing logically. How could you choose Petey Burch over me? Look at me--a brilliant student, a tremendous intellectual, a man with an assured future. Look at Petey--a knothead, a jitterbug, a guy who'll never know where his next meal is coming from . Can you give me one logical reason why you should go steady with Petey Burch?"

"I certainly can," declared Polly. "He's got a raccoon coat."

FALLACIES OF LOGIC

A fallacy is a piece of false reasoning. One of the keys to writing a successful research paper is to use logical persuasion. If your persuasion is based on false reasoning, your reader will perceive it, and your case will be lost. Therefore, it is important to recognize some of the fallacies which can lead you astray. Here is a list of eight common fallacies of logic with explanations and examples. Look for them in your reading; be careful not to create them in your writing.

Ad Misericordiam	An appeal to sympathy without presenting a logical argument.
	A student wants to run for Student Council President. When the advisor to the Student Council asks the student why she hasn't filed the proper petitions on time, she states: "I'm new in this school, and I don't have any friends, and my mother wants me to be President because she was when she was in school, and she thinks I should do everything she did, and I just want to be accepted, and so it's not my fault."
	(gag) This student didn't answer the question or present a logical answer to the question.
Contradictory Premises	When the statements on which an argument is based contradict each other, the argument cannot be made.
	If Zeus can do whatever he wants, can he create a lightning bolt so untouchably hot that he won't be able to throw it? If he can do whatever he wants, he should be able to throw it. But if it is untouchably hot, he won't be able to make it. But if he can do whatever he wants, he should be able to make it.
Dicto Simpliciter	An argument based on an unqualified generalization.
	Chewing gum is good. Everyone should chew gum.
	You must qualify the generalization.
	People with braces are told by their dentists not to chew gum. Sugared gum can promote cavities. Some people look horrible when they chew gum.
	Chewing gum is *usually* good.

False Analogy	An incorrect comparison is made between two things that are not alike.
	Since students have teachers to show them how to do their work in school, lawyers should have judges show them how to win their case in court.

	The two situations are completely different. The lawyer is already supposed to know the law and how to run a legal case. The student isn't supposed to know everything yet.
Hasty Generalization	The generalization is arrived at too quickly; there isn't enough evidence.
	I can't cook Chinese. Mary can't cook Chinese. Jenny can't cook Chinese. Therefore, I deduce that no one in Racine can cook Chinese.
	There are too few examples to support the generalization.
Hypothesis Contrary to Fact	An untrue beginning hypothesis cannot produce any reasonable deductions.
	If the Challenger had not blown up, Christa McCauliffe would still be alive and well today.
	You cannot know what would have happened if the Challenger had not blown up. Any number of things could have happened to Christa in the meantime.
Poisoning the Well	To cripple an opponent before the contest begins.
	Two candidates for Student Council Treasurer each have an opportunity to give a campaign speech on the school public announcement system. The first candidate starts by saying that the other candidate cheated on a math test, never did his homework, missed a lot of school and thinks the campaign is just a popularity contest.
	The opponent hasn't even got a chance. It isn't fair.
Post Hoc	The conclusion is drawn from a cause and effect relationship that doesn't exist.
	Every time we go to the movies with Nick Dismore, it's sold out. So we don't take Nick to the movies with us anymore.
	Nick doesn't cause the movie theater to be sold out. There is no connection between the two things. You can't blame Nick for the situation.

METHODS OF DEVELOPMENT

Information from your sources will vary quite a bit. Sometimes your summary or paraphrase will follow the exact same method of developing ideas. You should learn to recognize and reproduce the following ways of logically presenting information.

1. **EXEMPLIFICATION**

    When you have several examples that prove your point, you should specifically write them, presenting first the least important example and moving to the most important.

    For example:

    Cigarette smoking is bad for you. It discolors your skin and teeth. It gives you bad breath. It increases the possibility of illnesses like bronchitis, emphysema and cancer. It can kill you.

2. **COMPARISON/CONTRAST**

    When you compare two or more things, you are looking at their similarities or the things they have in common. When you contrast two or more things, you are discovering their differences. Those things *which are different* help you decide which product is the best. You can list similarities and differences in least to most important order.

    There are two methods of developing a comparison/contrast: the Item-By-Item Method, in which you discuss the characteristics of each in an alternating way, (first A, then B, then A, then B, etc.) and the Block Method, in which you discuss all the characteristics of one (A) and then all the characteristics of the other (B). You must maintain a parallel structure in the comparison/contrast. In either method, **mention last the one you think is best**. For example:

    Item-By-Item:

    Uncle Benito's pizza has three different sizes, and so does Pizza Place. At Uncle Benito's, breadsticks and sauce are available. Pizza Place has both also. Uncle Benito's prices are reasonable, and Pizza Place's are as well. However, Uncle Benito's pizza sauce is too sweet, but Pizza Place's is kind of tangy. Although Uncle Benito's offers a wide variety of pizzas, Pizza Place offers sandwiches and traditional Italian food, like spaghetti, as well as a salad bar. Uncle Benito's is carryout or delivery only whereas Pizza Place offers a third choice: family style dining at a restaurant, with red and white checked table cloths, placemats with games and puzzles on them for the children, and a juke box.

Here is the Block Method example:

Uncle Benito's pizza has three different sizes, breadsticks and sauce, and its prices are reasonable. However, Uncle Benito's pizza sauce is too sweet, and no other kinds of foods are on the menu. Uncle Benito's offers the convenience of carryout and delivery.

Pizza Place also has three different sizes, breadsticks and sauce, and quite reasonable prices. But Pizza Place's pizza sauce is kind of tangy. When people feel like something else, however, Pizza Place offers a menu of other traditional Italian meals, like spaghetti, as well as a salad bar. They also offer a third option: family style dining in, with red and white checked tablecloths, placemats with games and puzzles for the children, and a juke box.

3.   **CAUSE AND EFFECT**

Life is full of cause and effect relationships. They usually can be categorized in one of three ways: One cause with many effects, many causes with one effect, or a causal chain, in which each effect becomes the cause of another effect, as in a chain reaction.

<u>**One Cause with many effects**</u>:

A tornado swept through Naperville, Illinois, two days before school opened in August. The school was destroyed, students had to transfer to other schools, and the community had to find ways to provide for people who lost their homes. Some people died.

<u>**Many causes with one major effect**</u>:

The world had been suffering a decade-long financial depression. Nationalism in Germany was on the rise. A charismatic leader came to power in Germany, Adolph Hitler, and he wanted Germany to become more wealthy and powerful. Other countries of the world did not want another world war, so they did not act strongly and decisively. Then Hitler's armies invaded Poland and World War II began.

<u>**Causal chain**</u>:

Last night I stayed up late watching TV. Because of that I woke up so late I almost missed the bus, and I left my homework at home. Because I left my homework at home, I got a zero in class. Because I got a zero in class (my third), the teacher called my mom at work. Because of my bad grade, and the teacher interrupting my mom at work, Mom was very angry with me. I don't get to watch TV on school nights as my punishment.

4.   **DEFINITION**

There are two kinds of Definition. One is Denotative: it gives the dictionary meaning. If you are explaining technical terms in your paper, you will use the dictionary meaning. The other is Connotative: it gives the emotion and feeling of something, often with the use of figurative language, such as metaphor, simile or personification. Because a research paper is based mostly on logic and facts, a connotative definition is much less likely used.

Denotative:	Eating chocolate releases *endorphins*, which are endogenous opioid polypeptide compounds that resemble opiates in their abilities to produce a sense of well-being.
Connotative:	Eating chocolate can produce an *"endorphin rush"* which is another way of saying producing happy neurotransmitters, which reduce stress and lead to feelings of euphoria. No wonder J. K. Rowling used chocolate as a "medicine" to be distributed to injured wizards!

5.   ANALYSIS AND CATEGORIZATION

Sometimes a topic is so large and complex we need to analyze it, that is, break it down into parts. Once we have the major parts (which we can also call categories), we can determine to which category details belong.

It is not enough to give a definition of a research paper; we have to analyze the process, divide it into categories or break it down into smaller parts. For example, look at the timeline page of your book. The process is divided into weeks, which then lists specific lessons and assignments.

6.   PROBLEM AND SOLUTION

Some research papers are based on clearly specific problems, and your job is to provide clearly researched, logical, workable solutions to the problem. For example,

In our consumer-oriented, throw-away society, Americans are becoming more and more aware of filled-to-capacity landfills, and they recognize the costly problems they are producing: the need to purchase more land for waste disposal or to pay another municipality to take it, toxic run-off and waste, and the misuse of natural resources. The solutions are less obvious and difficult: We need to be better, more responsible consumers: we must demand less packaging, provide and use safer, more convenient methods of disposal for toxic products, and enact a greater commitment to recycling.

7.   SYNTHESIS

When you take ideas and information from many sources, and add in your own imagination, and from your own inspiration create a new complex idea or product, or a more elaborate outcome, you have synthesized.

Writing a research paper with your own original opinion expressed in a *thesis* and supported by many well-documented, logically connected sources is a synthesis.

WAYS TO CONCLUDE

You should restate your thesis in your conclusion, either exactly as it was in the introduction, or differently, perhaps with more impact. This is especially important in a long paper because by the time your readers get to the end, they may need a refresher that ties together all of your major and minor supporting details. Hopefully, you have done such an excellent job of logically developing your ideas and providing transitions between them that your reader will be right on target with you.

After this restatement, you may conclude your paper a number of different ways. A summary of your main points is certainly acceptable, but it is also the weakest of conclusions. After all, your reader just read those same points: repetition can be boring, and even insulting.

Perhaps, instead, you may **make a call for action** from your reader, based on the urgency of the information you have presented--you may ask them to write or call a congresswoman, or the mayor, or a school board member. You may wish to **end with a poignant quotation or poem** that finishes off the feelings of the paper. Just remember that your conclusion must be based on your data and that it should help persuade your reader to accept your thesis. The conclusion is not the place to provide new information.

Here are additional ways to develop a conclusion. Student samples illustrate them.

Make a prediction based on your research

> If world leaders such as the United States do not stop deforestation, global warming will be the destruction of the planet.—Clayton Gustin

State your opinion of the significance of your thesis

> The significance of ending Affirmative Action is obvious: reverse discrimination will continue to fuel the fires of prejudice that negatively affect us all.—Logan Reid

Answer the question(s) the paper asks

> Who is the greatest hockey player of all time? Lemieux!—Kyle Hayes

Offer the best solution to the problem posed

> The best solution to prevent the problems teenage pregnancies produce is to offer early education and birth control.—Ashley Jackson

Cite alarming statistics which may move your reader to action

The murder rate of black males in the USA today is 1 in 27 whereas the murder rate of white females is 1 in 356. We must stop the violence!—Elizabeth Gordon

Illustrate the problem with a short narrative of someone's experience and ask the question it demands (which, of course, is answered by your thesis!)

Christy Henrich's lengthy and losing battle to sports-driven anorexia nervosa and bulimia makes the answer to the question "What can we do to stop this?" obvious. For their safety and self-esteem, we must stop abusive practices against girls involved in gymnastics.—Mary Blandford

WRITING A SENTENCE OUTLINE

Once you have completed your Preliminary Outline, and you are well satisfied that it is in the correct order to persuade your readers, and you believe you have thoroughly covered each subtopic with enough specific details and with correct parenthetical documentation, NOW you are ready to write your SENTENCE OUTLINE. Beginning on a new page, write or type your introductory paragraph, including the specific sentences and parenthetical documentation. Without it, you will not be able to check that your paper has made all your major points and that the structure is parallel. Just the headings Hook, Thesis and Functional Introduction will not be enough. Be sure you follow the rules given in the directions on the previous page.

When you begin the second Roman Numeral, you will need to refer constantly to your Functional Introduction, your Preliminary Outline and to your resources, which, hopefully you have highlighted and underlined well, and which you have marked already to determine if the material you will use will be written as a summary, a paraphrase or a direct quotation. Remember, you want to achieve a balance of those methods, but <u>they each have a specific purpose and meaning</u>, so don't just decide on writing in a cycle of summary, paraphrase, quote, summary, paraphrase, quote, etc.! Your writing will be more sophisticated if you provide that variety, but only if you do it appropriately. AGAIN, YOU MUST CARRY FORWARD TO THIS OUTLINE THE PARENTHETICAL DOCUMENTATION INFORMATION AFTER EACH SOURCE YOU USE. DON'T LOSE IT NOW!

Here is an example of Matt Tomkins' Sentence Outline on Jackie Robinson. Note that the parts of the Functional Introduction are in [brackets], and note the (parenthetical documentation) is in parentheses and the periods or commas are correctly placed. Be sure you follow this example.

I.   Introduction

      A.   (Hook.) Before 1946, African-Americans were not allowed to play in professional baseball. By battling his way into an all white league, Jackie Robinson became one of the best baseball players ever.

      B.   (Thesis.) Jackie Robinson changed professional sports.

      C.   (Functional Introduction.)

            [1] A remarkably talented African-American of the 1940's and 1950's,

            [2] Jackie Robinson's recruitment into the previously all white league

            [3] led him into a fight for racial equality.

            [4] This brave man's life had a positive impact on American society.

II. Jackie Robinson was famous for his athletic talent.

    A. His pre-professional baseball statistics were accomplished in both high school and junior college.

        1. While attending Muir High School in Pasadena, Jackie Robinson earned letters in football, baseball, basketball, and track (LoCurto 2).

        2. Jackie then attended Pasadena Junior College. There he led his football team to 11 straight victories, and to a win over Compton College in the 1939 Rose Bowl (3).

        3. Edwin (Duke) Snider, who was later one of Jackie's Dodger teammates, was watching the game. He recalls, "Jackie was great in football, basketball, and baseball. He could have been a pro in all three sports" (12).

        4. At a track meet on 8 May 1939, Robinson pole vaulted 15'6 1/2" to break his brother's national junior college record. He then jumped into a waiting car and went to a Glendale baseball diamond to lead his baseball team to a 5 to 3 victory to win the Southern California junior college baseball championship (12).

        5. He remains U.C.L.A.'s only four sport letterman (12).

    B. In the Minor Leagues Jackie added significantly to his statistics.

        1. In 1946, Jackie Robinson played for a farm team of the Dodgers, the Montreal Royals, of the International League (Meyer 40).

        2. He batted .349 to win the batting title, led the league in stolen bases with 40, and had 133 runs (40).

        3. On the field, Jackie had a league-leading .985 fielding average, making only 10 errors. He had 261 putouts and 385 assists (40).

    C. Even in his first year his accomplishments were remarkable.

        1. In 1947, Jackie was promoted to the Brooklyn Dodgers. During that year, he proved that he had a lot of athletic talent (Knudson 10).

        2. He batted .297 and had 12 home runs in 151 games, and won the first of two stolen base titles with 29 thefts (11).

        3. As a reward for having a great year, and for contributing to the Dodger's winning the National League pennant, Robinson was voted Rookie of the Year (12).

        Et cetera

STYLE . . . .
WHO SAID, HE SAID SHE SAID?

One of the goals we are aiming for is a more sophisticated writing style, much of which depends on *varying sentence length* and *word choice*. Word Choice, also referred to as Diction, can mean using concrete and often proper nouns to give the reader something more solid to hold on to, and thus to better understand what the writer is saying. For you, the writer, this is a great time to begin to grow and stretch your style by experimenting with new words, both for clarity and interest. Which of the following sentences means more? Why do you think so?

She said that he said that she said she was innocent.

In her article, she reported that he had stated for the record that she claimed her complete innocence.

In her news article, Hill reported that defending attorney Brown stated for the record that his client Ms. Jones claimed she was innocent of all charges.

The first short sentence uses pronouns for which we have no identity and uses the same verb three times. We don't know what is going on!

The second sentence varies the verb and is more accurate and more specific than just "said," but it still doesn't give us enough information.

The third sentence provides us with names and descriptions of the people, as well as giving us the variation on the verbs that is much more specific. Now we know what is going on!

As writers and speakers, our intelligence and experience are expressed through our vocabulary, and we are judged by our word choice. If we want to be taken seriously, we have to use words seriously. Have you ever seen the science fiction movie called *Space Camp*? One of the characters is an incredibly brilliant girl named Trish, but she is considered a bimbo by most of the other characters because of the way she talks and dresses like a Valley Girl. She purposely dumbs herself down to be socially accepted. Don't make the same mistake in your writing. Aim high!

STYLE . . . OTHER WAYS TO SAY SAYS

One of the problems in writing research papers is the way in which we introduce information from other sources. There are a lot of ways to say "says." On the next pages is an alphabetical list of over 200 ways to say "says." Personalize this list by marking words you already frequently use in your own vocabulary with a star. Put a check next to words you have heard but don't use. Circle the words that are new to you. Look them up to understand their contextual meaning. Now you have your own, personalized vocabulary list of words to try out.

Be careful that the word you use to say "says" in writing your paper matches the contextual meaning of the rest of each sentence and does not sound artificial, or pushed. Remember, too, that your word choice reflects your tone or your attitude toward your subject and your audience. **Don't just throw any word into a sentence because you need a word that means "says." It has to fit in meaning and in tone in order to reflect the right style for you.** Vary your sentence length and be sure to give enough information.

1. acclaim	21. asks	41. cites
2. according to	22. assumes	42. claims
3. accuses	23. assures	43. clarifies
4. acknowledges	24. attests	44. commands
5. adds	25. barks	45. commences
6. admits	26. begins	46. commends
7. advertises	27. begs	47. comments
8. advises	28. believes	48. compares
9. affirms	29. bellows	49. complains
10. agrees	30. blasts	50 compliments
11. alarms	31. blurts (out)	51. compromises
12. alleges	32. boasts	52. concedes
13. analyzes	33. brags	53. concurs
14. announces	34. calculates	54. confirms
15. answers	35. cautions	55. congratulates
16. anticipates	36. challenges	56. confesses
17. apologizes	37. charges	57. considers
18. applauds	38. chirps	58. contemplates
19. approves	39. chokes	59. contends
20. argues	40. chuckles	60. contests

61. continues	99. groans	137. preaches
62. contradicts	100. grumbles	138. predicts
63. corrects	101. guesses	139. prescribes
64. counsel	102. hesitates	140. presumes
65. counters	103. hopes	141. proclaims
66. counters	104. hypothesizes	142. professes
67. cries	105. implies	143. projects
68. criticizes	106. infers	144. promises
69. debates	107. informs	145. pronounces
70. declares	108. inquires	146. proposes
71. defends	109. insists	147. protests
72. defines	110. invites	148. queries
73. deliberates	111. interjects	149. questions
74. demands	112. interrupts	150. quips
75 disagrees.	113. jokes	151. quotes
76. disapproves	114. laughs	152. rambles
77. disclaims	115. maintains	153. rationalizes
78. discloses	116. marvels	154. reaffirms
79. disputes	117. mentions	155. realizes
80. drawls	118. moans	156. reasons
81. drones	119. mocks	157. reassures
82. echoes	120. mumbles	158. recalls
83. elucidates	121. murmurs	159. recommends
84. emphasizes	122. notes	160. reiterates
85. encourages	123. notices	161. relates
86. estimates	124. observes	162. remarks
87. expects	125. offers	163. remembers
88. explains	126. opposes	164 reminds
89. feels	127. orders	165. reminisces
90. forbids	128. outlines	166. repeats
91. forecasts	129. pants	167. replies
92. foresees	130. perceives	168. reports
93. foretells	131. persists	169. reprimands
94. forewarns	132. philosophizes	170. reproaches
95. frets	133. pleads	171. requests
96. gasps	134. pledges	172. retorts
97. generalizes	135. points out	173. retracts
98. gripes	136. ponders	174. reveals
175. reviews	188. steams	201. theorizes
176. scoffs	189. stipulates	202. thinks

177. scolds	190. storms	203. threatens
178. scorns	191. stresses	204. translates
179. screams	192. stutters	205. verbalizes
180. sighs	193. substitutes	206. verifies
181. snaps	194. supports	207. voices
182. sobs	195. surmises	208. warns
183. soothes	196. supposes	209. welcomes
184. specifies	197. sympathizes	210. whispers
185 speculates	198. tells	211. wishes
186. stammers	199. testifies	212. worries
187. states	200. thanks	213. yells

STYLE . . . TRANSITIONS: CONNECTING LANGUAGE

One of your goals as a research paper writer is to make it easy for your audience to go smoothly from one idea to the next. Sophisticated writers provide certain words and phrases that help make the relationships between ideas clear and logical. There are three well known methods for providing these logical and smooth transitions from one idea to the next.

One way to show the connections is to **repeat key words and phrases** from one paragraph in the next paragraph. The repetition gives the reader an understood concept to hold onto as new material is presented.

Another way is to **use old information to introduce new information**, in a kind of building process; or you could use it as beginning with something familiar, and by comparison, moving to something unfamiliar. An example of this would be in coaxing someone who is familiar with typewriters and who eats out a lot to use a computer. Begin with the familiar keyboard, and the concept of a menu.

The most obvious way to make connections is to **use words called transitional markers**. They are placed at or near the beginning of a sentence to indicate the relationship to the preceding sentence. Sometimes they are used as conjunctions in combining sentences. Beware of overdoing it! Make sure you understand the meaning and implication of the word to the relationship between two ideas before you use it. Try out some new connecting language to improve the sophistication of your writing.

Here is a list of transitional markers categorized by their purposes:

TO INDICATE ADDITION (listing)

> again, also, and, and then, besides, equally important, finally, first, further, furthermore, in addition, last, likewise, moreover, next, second, third, too

TO INDICATE CAUSE AND EFFECT

> accordingly, as a result, consequently, hence, in short, otherwise, then, therefore, thus, truly

TO INDICATE COMPARISON (similarities)

> in a like manner, likewise, similarly

TO INDICATE CONCESSION (opposing or refuting evidence)

after all, although this may be true, at the same time, even though, admittedly, naturally, of course, obviously

TO INDICATE CONTRAST (differences)

after all, although it's true that, and yet, at the same time, but for all that, however, in contrast, in spite of, nevertheless, notwithstanding, on the contrary, on the other hand, still, yet

TO INDICATE SPECIAL FEATURES, REASONS OR EXAMPLES (exemplification)

for example, for instance, incidentally, indeed, in fact, in other words, in particular, specifically, that is, to illustrate

TO INDICATE SUMMARY (repeat)

in brief, in conclusion, in short, on the whole, to conclude, to summarize, to sum up

TO INDICATE TIME RELATIONSHIPS (narration)

after a short time, afterwards, as long as, as soon as, at last, at length, at that time, at the same time, before, earlier, immediately, in the meantime, lately, later, meanwhile, of late, presently, shortly, since, soon, temporarily, thereafter, thereupon, until, when, while

STYLE . . . WHAT DO YOU SAY TO WHOM, AND HOW?

Your writing style is personal, but it is developed in much the same way as everyone else's. Your background has a definite influence on your writing style. It is influenced by your age, home, family, experiences, gender, education, travel, hobbies, as well as the amount and kind of TV and movies you watch. But most of all, surprise, surprise: Your writing style is greatly affected by how much and what you have read! Here are some elements that affect a person's writing style:

Using standard or nonstandard vocabulary

Having a positive or a negative slant or attitude toward your subject

Writing short direct sentences (under ten words); long, combined sentences (over thirty words); or a combination of short, medium, and long sentences

Employing specific, concrete words, or subtle, abstract ones

Making comparisons that use metaphors and similes and other figurative language, or using no imagery

Creating a tone that is sincere and direct, or genuinely humorous, or sarcastic, etc.

Exhibiting an overall cautious attitude toward the subject and/or the audience, a neutral attitude toward the subject and/or the audience, or an assertive attitude toward the topic and/or the audience

Which of the above elements will be appropriate in a research paper? Why?

Remember, your writing style is just as personal as your hair style or clothes sense; it is not better or worse than anyone else's; it's just different! And that's good! But you should be aware that even you will change your style depending on circumstances, and that is appropriate and important.

STYLE EXERCISE NUMBER ONE: Here is an exercise to see the difference in your style depending on the person to whom you are speaking. You will undoubtedly see that you don't always tell the same story the same way!

The class will number off and be in groups of fours. All the number one's within each group should meet together to brainstorm a good (fictional) sob story of the details of their recent breakup with the person they have been dating. If that's not comfortable, make it the best friend they've just discovered has been backstabbing them. The other group members should number off, two, three and four, and decide a role they each plan to play from any of the following possibilities: the mother of the storyteller, a younger sibling, a best friend, the best friend of the person you've lost, a minister, your English teacher, your psychiatrist.

After only five minutes of preparation, the one's should rejoin their group consisting of a two, three and a four. Number two, identify your role and ask for the story. Number one, play up the part well--have fun dramatizing! After one minute, number three takes over, announcing his/her role. Start the story over. After another minute, number four takes over, announcing his/her role. Start the story over. Two's, three's and four's may play up their role as much as they want. Keep going around the group until the story and all its vivid details are out in the open. **STOP.**

Now in your small groups discuss what happened. Appoint a recorder to write down your answers. Did the number one's change in the way they spoke? Did they become secretive or evasive with certain listener's roles? Did they get louder or use more emphatic language? How did their diction change? How about the amount of information they were willing to give depending on the person to whom they were talking? What does this exercise show you about your writing style in relationship to your audience? How will it affect your writing in the research paper? After this short discussion of five minutes or so, appoint a reporter from your group to tell the whole class your discoveries.

STYLE EXERCISE NUMBER TWO: Here is another exercise which you can do in class with a partner. Establish who will be the COMPLAINER and who will be the RESPONDER. Complainer, you have an important problem: you need quiet! Maybe you have a big exam to study for; maybe you have a sick child in the house; maybe you are baby-sitting for a baby who has finally gone to sleep after hours of crying; maybe you've just come back from a slumber party at which no one slumbered! Whatever! But the person in the apartment next door, on the other side of the paper thin wall, has just started to play his stereo at full blast, and his three dogs are running and barking in the half-bathroom where they've been trapped. You need the noise to stop! Responder, you are going to change roles every minute, in the following order: the next door stereo man, the building manager, and the police. As the complainer begins to whine, responder should react, and then change roles, one minute each. After five minutes, **STOP.**

Discuss with your partner the different styles of communicating that the complainer used. Discuss the tone of voice and volume the complainer used depending on the different audience he or she had. How can you express tone of voice and volume with the written word in a research paper? What have you learned about the effect of an audience on your written style? Share your answers with your class.

How could this principle apply to your writing?

STYLE . . . TONE: IT'S MY ATTITUDE

Because words can have different meanings, either by their dictionary definitions, which are called Denotative, or by the emotional responses they carry for the writer and create in the reader, which are called Connotative, word choice can also affect the way you express your ideas. And that will affect the way your reader understands you. It's the expression of your attitude--whether it is directed toward your subject or toward your audience.

In the style exercises you have done, along with your tone of voice, your volume, your gestures and your speed of speaking, you used different words to carry your overall feelings and meanings about your particular predicament. In writing, you cannot rely on the tone of voice, the volume, the gestures and speed; none of that will be there for the reader. Thus the reader must get a feeling for your meaning solely from your words and punctuation. Achieving that is sometimes a really difficult process for the writer. A good vocabulary and an ear for language really make a difference in what a writer can accomplish. Again, this is a good reason to become an avid reader--expose yourself to as many ideas and words as you can and develop that ear!

Here is an example of feedback comments written on an assignment by a teacher. What does each comment really mean? Which comment would you rather receive?

1. "This report is not at all what I expected from you."

2. "This report is terrible."

3. "Your report shows promise, but it is not, as yet, up to passing standards."

4. "Your report is a slovenly disgrace."

5. "Your report is one sandwich short of a picnic, one brick short of a load. It shows that the light is on, but no one is home. In other words, it is incomplete."

Well, perhaps you chose the last set of comments because they exhibit a sense of humor, which is indeed, a TONE, but they are also all insulting. These expressions, called EUPHEMISMS (ways of saying something indirectly, perhaps softening the blow, so to speak), can also get you in a lot of trouble in writing a research paper because this particular kind of writing, which is supposed to be sophisticated, sincere, and persuasive, is not funny, cute or misleading. Choose the direct, honest words if you want a reader to trust you.

STYLE . . . WHAT'S APPROPRIATE?

When you think of TONE in writing, think of the words that describe human moods. What words do you want to choose to express your attitudes toward your subject and your readers in writing your research paper? To find out, do the following exercise.

Read over the following list. Put a check mark next to the words you already know. Some of these words may be new to you. Look up their meanings in a dictionary and write the definition in your own words next to them. Next, circle the words you think would be appropriate to describe the kinds of TONE you would expect to use in your research paper. Finally, in a small group, discuss why you would use certain tones, and avoid others.

_____simple	_____serious
_____straightforward	_____solemn
_____direct	_____indifferent
_____unambiguous	_____jovial
_____complicated	_____easy
_____complex	_____friendly
_____difficult	_____unconcerned
_____forceful	_____hopeless
_____powerful	_____hopeful
_____ironic	_____consistent
_____sardonic	_____accepting
_____sarcastic	_____hostile
_____indirect	_____critical
_____understated	_____evasive
_____bitter	_____grim
_____sympathetic	_____interested
_____apathetic	_____antagonistic
_____outraged	_____indignant
_____angry	_____elevated
_____grand	_____respectful

Finally, discuss among your small group what the effect of your tone will be on your audience. By the way, just who is your audience?

PUBLISHING INSTRUCTIONS FOR THE FINAL DRAFT

The way your final paper looks can make a difference in the way it is received. The paper you turn in should be neatly done, following the directions given below for the type of paper you use, the type of print or ink you use, for the way you write page numbers, and for the way you space your information. You, and only you, are responsible for the excellence of every part of your paper. For the amount of work that this project represents, you should make certain that you have no spelling, punctuation or capitalization errors. Your quotations, summaries and paraphrases should be completely and correctly documented. You should have adequate support, and your ideas should be presented in a logical order. Typed papers are preferred because they are neater and thus easier to read.

Whether you are writing your paper by hand or using a computer, be neat. If you are using a computer printer, make sure it you have a full ink cartridge, and an extra one handy. You don't want to run out of ink when an assignment is due the next day. Choose an **easy-to- read font or type** style. The size should be legible; try size 12 and check it with your instructor by showing him or her an example to make sure it is acceptable. If you are handwriting your paper, use dark blue or black ink. **USE ONLY ONE SIDE OF A PAGE.** The quality of the paper you use is important as well. Use a only white paper, 8 1/2 X 11 inches and 20 pound weight. If you are handwriting, use only white loose-leaf, lined paper.

Double-space your paper consistently throughout its entirety, including quotations and the list of Works Cited. Do not quadruple-space between paragraphs. Indenting alone signals a new paragraph.

It is very important for you to make a copy of your work, in case it gets lost or destroyed. No one *ever* wants to have to reconstruct an entire paper. If you are using a computer, make sure you save your work often throughout the process of writing, revision, and editing, and also make a back up copy on the hard drive, a disc or flash drive.

Whether typing or handwriting, *except for page numbers*, make sure you **keep one inch margins on all sides of your paper:** top, bottom, left and right. If you are using a computer, do not justify your lines. **Every paragraph should have the first line indented** five spaces from the left margin (one inch if handwritten). Long, direct quotations of more than four lines must be set off ten spaces **from the left margin only** (two inches if handwritten). Indent those same ten spaces (two inches) for every line of that set-off quotation. Double-space the lines within the set-off quotation; maintain the double-spacing before and after the long, set-off quotation--do not add more spaces.

Each instructor may have a different set of instructions for your title page, so pay attention to directions. According to the *MLA Handbook for Writers of Research Papers, 7th edition*, upon which this text is based, however, no separate title page is used. Instead, beginning one half inch down on the right side of the page, type your last name only and the number 1, indicating the first page, *so that it runs flush with the right hand margin.* Do not type the word "page" or an abbreviation for the word page, or any other symbol or punctuation mark. On every page that follows, you will type your last name and the page number (consecutively) in this same location. Be sure you do not type or write in the right hand margin! If you are typing, set a tab for this location. If your computer has a preset one inch margin, go to the menu item entitled "Page Setup" and make the adjustment to one-half inch for the top margin.

Next, spacing down another half inch (so now you are one inch from the top edge of the page, flush with the *left* margin, type your name, double-space down, type your instructor's name, double-space down, type the course or class name, double-space down, and type the date, European fashion (20 January 2009). Then, double-space down once more, and center the title of your paper. **<u>Do not underline your title. Do not put your title in quotation marks. Do not make your title in bold print. Do not put your title in all capital letters. Do not put a period at the end of your title.</u>** Then, double-space down again, indent five spaces or one inch and begin the introductory paragraph of your paper. *Your paper will have no subheadings except for the Works Cited page.* Employ the transition words you have learned to go from one idea to the next; if necessary, write a sentence or short paragraph to move from one part of your paper to the next.

A word to the wise about plastic covers and folders. Most instructors prefer to have the paper bound by a single staple in the upper left hand corner. The plastic covers are slippery and come apart; the folders just add weight to an already heavy briefcase! Unless your instructor suggests a plastic cover, folder or an illustrated title page, follow the directions for the title page above, and use the stapler.

TIPS ON WRITING YOUR RESEARCH PAPER

AVOID: Using I in your paper (also my, mine)

AVOID: Using You in your paper (No direct address; no second person voice)

AVOID: Abbreviations (Too informal)

AVOID: Contractions (Too informal)

AVOID: All slang, except in direct quotations. (Too informal)

AVOID: Starting a sentence with a numeral--you MUST write out the number in words (Thirty thousand, not 30,000)—you may start "About 30,000"

AVOID: Using first names of authors or authorities--it is sexist stereotyping

AVOID: Using just one example to draw a conclusion—Hasty Generalization

AVOID: Placing anything, even name and page number in the right hand margin.

AVOID: Writing "the reason why" or "The reason is because." BOTH are REDUNDANT, which is insulting and and repetitive. They all mean the same thing!

AVOID: Using a font that is too large (which makes it look like you are trying to stretch a paper that is too short and undeveloped) or too small (which makes it look like you have too much material for the assignment).

ALWAYS: Strike only one space after a colon.

ALWAYS: Strike a space after each period in an ellipsis.

ALWAYS: Strike two spaces after an end period, and one space after a comma

Use two hyphens to make a DASH--and use NO SPACE on either side of the DASH.

PARENTHETICAL DOCUMENTATION REMINDERS:

If you are using a Direct Quote, you must cite the EXACT page on which it is found. You may not give a range of pages of the entire article.

If you have two articles written by the same author: in the Works Cited, you must alphabetize by the author's last name, and then by the first letter of the first word of the title of the article or book.

In the parenthetical documentation, you must use the author's last name and at least the first three words of the article from which you are quoting, so the reader knows to which article you refer.

Before you turn in your paper, read through it carefully, page by page, to <u>make sure that every parenthetical documentation has a matching source citation on the Works Cited page</u>! If it doesn't, you must either not use it, or you must rewrite the Works Cited to include it. If you do it right the first time, you'll save time!

PEER CONFERENCING EVALUATION FORM

There are several purposes for peer conferencing. You will have an opportunity to have an audience for your work before it counts for a grade. Your partner will read your paper thoroughly for content and style, as well as for very specific questions, which are listed below. Your partner's purpose is not to tear your paper to pieces, but instead, to give you some constructive advice on how you can still improve it. Your partner will encourage you. From the experience of peer conferencing your partner's paper, you will become a better evaluator of your own work. You both will become more critical readers and better writers.

Before you exchange papers with a partner to peer conference, be sure you have made a copy of it so you won't mind having the partner write on it. To make identification of passages easier for both of you, number your paragraphs in the left hand margin of your paper.

Answer the following questions as specifically as possible, but to speed the process, use the first three words, only, of any passage you wish to point out or to which you want to refer, and include the paragraph number. Use a separate sheet of paper to answer these questions so that you can preserve this sheet as a form to follow in future peer conferences.

Evaluator's Name _____

Date _____

Author's Name _____

1.   Is the paper's title page correct?

        Is the paper properly typed with one inch margins?_____

        Is the paper properly double-spaced throughout? _____

        Is the Heading done according to directions?_____

        Is the title interesting? _____ Suggest a better one_____

        Is the title correctly placed and typed? _____

        Are the pages numbered correctly? _____

        Is the Works Cited correctly spaced? _____

        Is the Works Cited correctly alphabetized? _____

Is the parenthetical documentation punctuation correct?_____

Do the citations in Works Cited match the parenthetical documentation?

Are long quotations correctly set off?_____

2.   Write the Thesis Sentence and where it is located in the paper.

3.   Write out the Functional Introduction in outline form:

   A.

   B.

   C.

   D. etc.

4.   Is the Functional Introduction's order followed precisely in the paper?_____   If not, where is the error?_____

5.   According to the Functional Introduction, is anything missing from the paper? What?

6.   According to the Functional Introduction, is anything extra in the paper? What?

7.   Identify the author's Hook. Did it work? Can you suggest something better?

8.   List some of the transition words and phrases or devices the author used to connect the ideas in the paper.

9.   List places where better transitions are needed, page, paragraph, and line number.

10. Give specific examples of the way the author used any or all of the following types of development:

Definition

Least to Most Important Idea

Cause and Effect (one cause, many effects, or many causes with one effect, or causal chain reaction)

Comparison

Contrast

Exemplification (Develop by use of examples)

Problem/ Solution

Categorization

11. What did you find most interesting about the paper?

12. If you could, what would you have the author delete from the paper? Why?

13. If the author could fix part of this paper, what part would you recommend?

14. What questions would you like to ask the author that he or she could respond to, and then by adding the answers to the paper, make it better?

15. Please mark any spelling errors, capitalization errors, punctuation errors, and grammar errors you find in the paper.

SELF-EVALUATION SHEET

Your Name_____

In order to evaluate this research paper, you should be as specific as possible in answering the following questions. Answer them on another sheet of paper to preserve this form for future use.

1. What are you trying to say or prove in this research paper?

2. What kind of HOOK did you employ?

3. List (at least three) major points of support (subtopics) you have mentioned to support your thesis sentence in the introductory paragraph.

    a._____

    b._____

    c._____

    d._____

    e._____

4. Give specific examples from your paper that used any of the following types of development.

    Definition_____

    _____

    Least to Most Important Idea_____

    _____

    Cause and Effect Relationship_____

    _____

    Comparison_____

    _____

Contrast_____

_____

Exemplification_____

_____

Problem/Solution_____

_____

Categorization_____

_____

5. Does your paper employ parallel structure--does your paper's structure follow the same order as the Functional Introduction?_____ If not, what will you do to correct it?__

_____

6. Are your ideas tied together smoothly and logically with transitional markers?

List some you used._____

_____

Do you need to add any? _____

7. Have you parenthetically documented all direct quotations, all summaries and all paraphrases of material you used from resources?_____ Did you follow the Before and After Rules of Punctuation with your parenthetical documentation?_____ Do the page numbers in your parenthetical documentation match the page numbers listed in your Works Cited?_____

8. Have you completed your Works Cited list correctly? _____ Have you put the page number in the correct place? _____ Have you correctly titled the page?_____ Have you alphabetized by the authors' last names?____ Have you indented second and subsequent lines of entries?_____ **Have you double spaced throughout?**_____

9. Does your conclusion pull together your entire paper and support or restate your thesis? _____ What method of concluding did you use?

_____

10. What do you like best in your paper?_____

_____

11. What can you do to make your entire paper that good?_____

_____

12. What do you like least in your paper?_____

_____

Should you delete it or improve it?_____ Do you need more

information?_____

13. What would you work on if you had 24 hours more to spend on writing your

paper?_____

14. If you could do this project over, what would you change about what you did?

Topic_____   Library time_____   Varying Resources More_____

Thesis Sentence_____   Outlining_____   Transitions_____

Functional Introduction_____   Reading time_____   Rewriting_____

Use of class time_____   Homework time_____   Getting a computer_____

Revising/Rewriting work as it is done_____   Documenting_____

Keeping to the timeline schedule_____

When you write your next research paper, revisit this page; it tells you what advice you've given yourself to do a better job. Pay attention to your recommendations!

CHRONOLOGICAL LIST OF STUDENT ASSIGNMENTS

1. Write a list of three topics on which you think you could write. Discuss them with others.

2. Make a final choice and have your parent sign it. Hand this in for a grade.

3. Fill out the "Questions, questions. . ." sheet and hand it in for a grade.

4. Read the entire section on preparing the Works Cited to become familiar with it.

5. Do the two Works Cited Exercises, using the Rules and Examples section, and hand it in for grades.

6. (Before going to the library, you might do an exercise on the use of the Reader's Guide.)

7. Make your own Working Bibliography with an initial **minimum** of 20 to 25 reference citations. You will add to this as you proceed with your paper.

8. Do the Summary Exercise.

9. Do the Paraphrase Exercise.

10. Gather sources. Go back to the libraries to work independently.

11. Read and highlight sources for main ideas. Write notes on photocopies. Be a Spider.

12. Read the section "(Parenthetical Documentation)."

13. Have the teacher check the total number of Citations you have on your Working Bibliography. This will help you from procrastinating.

14. Plan to show your teacher all the sources you have gathered to this point for a grade.

15. Continue to gather, read, and highlight sources. Write notes and connections on them.

16. Write three possible thesis sentences for your topic for group discussion.

17. Write the best possible thesis sentence you can.

18. Pre-write the Functional Introduction by drawing the several boxes, writing in your subtopics, and numbering them in a logical order.

19. Write a good, solid, logical Functional Introduction .

20.   Write the Introductory Paragraph to your paper including the Hook, the Thesis Sentence, and the Functional Introduction. Include any necessary Parenthetical Documentation.

21.   Start work on the Preliminary Outline by transferring information from your articles to the outline pages; turn it in at the beginning of Week Seven.

22.   Construct your Concluding Paragraph, due the end of Week Eight.

23.   Read through the Methods of Development again and make some plans for presenting your information in sentence and paragraph format.

24.   Write the Sentence Outline, due the first day of Week Nine.

25.   Write the rough draft of your Works Cited or type it on your computer and save it. Review the Rules; ask your teacher for help, if necessary. Turn in for a grade.

26.   Type/Write the final draft of your Works Cited to turn in for a grade.

27.   Begin writing your paper's rough draft as soon as you receive your graded Sentence Outline. Rough Drafts are due at the beginning of Week Ten in order to do Peer Conferencing.

28.   Revise and Edit your rough draft each night to prepare for class the next day.

29.   Rewrite your Works Cited immediately and turn it in so you can correct it before adding it to the end of your paper.

30.   Write/Type the final copy of your paper. Save it to a flash drive, hard drive, or disc. Make a second copy.

Ceremony and celebration!

Courtney Carlson's Research Paper Outline

The Disadvantaged Only Child: Fact or Fiction?

I. Introductory Paragraph
   A. Hook—Narrative example
   B. Thesis: There are many positive benefits of being an only child
   C. Functional Introduction
      1. Negative stereotypes
      2. Child psychologists' studies
      3. Positive personality traits not evident in children of large families
      4. Higher achievement and intelligence in "onlies"
      5. Specific examples of only children that illustrate statistical evidence
II. Negative Stereotypes of only children
   A. Negative view traced to G. Stanley Hall (Kutner and Singer 109)
      1. most doctoral students studied Hall (Sanders 25)
   B. Disadvantaged without siblings (Goode 50)
      1. Self-centered
      2. unhappy
      3. anxious
      4. demanding
      5. pampered
      6. maladjusted
   C. Parents also stereotyped as neurotic, selfish, materialistic (Day 755)
   D. Undesirable and detrimental to society (755
   E. Reason to have another child is to prevent the first from being an only (Sanders 24)
   F. Gallop Poll statistics (McGrath 19)
   G. Blake: being an only child is a serious handicap (210)
   H. Disadvantage suffered by only children is prejudice from teachers, neighbors, relatives (19,21)
III. More Recent Child Studies
   A. Falbo finds selfish and lonely is gross exaggeration (Goode 50)
   B. Psychologists start to question past practice (Kutner and Singer 110)
IV. Positive Personality Traits
   A. Not greedy or grabbing; able to share (Kiev and Sidar 46)
      1. Pampered lonely misfit theory is a myth (Katz 199)
      2. Explanation for spoiling is parents (Koontz 57)
      3. Wealth is a factor in spoiling (57)
      4. Social class is a factor (57)
      5. Myths disproved by prominent psychologist…"only children . . . clearly more advantaged than children from larger sib-sizes" (Day 755)
         a. receive a larger portion of parents' income
         b. have no competition for parental attention
         c. more time to themselves (755)

B. Only children develop very close friendships (Katz 199)
    1.   good social skills
    2.   ability to communicate well with peers (Katz 199)
C. Rated well above norm in sociability in terms of peer popularity (Kantrowitz and Greenberg 67)
    1.   majority of time spent with adults
    2.   one-on-one interaction
    3.   mature social skills
    4.   superior communication skills (Polit and Falbo 312)
    5.   Socially sophisticated
        a. participate in extracurricular activities
            1. sports
            2. student leadership (Kantrowitz and Greenberg 67)
D. Only children are "as well or better adjusted" than other children in their sense of control over their lives (Sanders 25)
E. Leadership; independence and self-reliance (Polit and Falbo 25)
F. Effects on adult life
    1.   Higher achieving in work life
    2.   Marry better educated spouses and have fewer children (25)
G. Creativity
    1.   Many grow up to be actors or artists
H. Greater amount of "character" due to more attention from parents (Polit and Falbo 25)
    1.   maturity
    2.   cooperativeness(25)
I. Higher Self-Confidence, independence, innovativeness, tolerance (Day 757)

V.   Achievement
A. Better grades
B. Higher goals
C. Earn more advanced academic degrees
D. Higher self-esteem (Koontz 56)
E. Higher scoring on intelligence tests than children from sibling groups (Sanders 25)
F. Skip a grade
G. Self-esteem and achievement motivation very high (Heil 102; Polit and Falbo 309)
H. Verbal and quantitative ability scores consistently higher in onlies (Kutner and Singer 110)
I. Only children receive twenty percent more education than children from larger families (Brophy 54)
J. Onlies scored highest on verbal IQ test . . . an excellent indicator of future academic success
K. "Every year, I ask my medical students . . . 85% are onlies or firstborns" (Brophy 54)

VI.   Specific Examples
    A. Creative spark "Onlies have more of a sense of creating their own worlds than other kids" Slung (Brophy 54)
    B. Performers and artists: Ansel Adams, Ezra Pound, Lillian Hellman, John Updike, Truman Capote, Elvis Presley, Ingrid Bergman, Cary Grant, Frank Sinatra, Leonardo da Vinci (54, 55)
    C. Time alone and separation beneficial to only children: in groups they "tend to dominate" (Brophy 54)
    D. Natural leadership in politics: Joseph Stalin, Indira Ghandi, Franklin Delano Roosevelt (Brophy)
VII.   Being brought up an "only" has many benefits.
    A. We are all "a part of those whom we have met"—Shakespeare (Sanders 25)

When you read Carlson's paper on the next pages, can you tell that it is following the structure of her outline?

You will see very small print in bold italics that analyzes all the parts of Carlson's paper: you will see the methods of development, and how the examples correspond to the outline. When you write your own paper, it will not have these notes on them.

Courtney Carlson

Mrs. Blandford

Accelerated English 8, Group 2

12 April 1996

<u>*TITLE*</u>   The Disadvantaged only Child: Fact or Fiction?

<u>*I.A. BEGINNING OF INTRODUCTION and HOOK and NARRATIVE EXAMPLE*</u>

A twenty-five year old woman pushes her young daughter in a stroller through the mall. An older woman stops her to talk to the baby. The woman reaches in the stroller and tickles the child.

"Do you have any brothers or sisters, sweetheart?" she coos.

"No—she is our only one."

Without stopping to think, the woman rambles on. "Is there something wrong with this one that you decided not to have any more? I hope you are planning on having more children. Do you know what only children can be like? They are selfish and spoiled, just to name a few things."

The young mother is speechless. She is so angry with this obviously ignorant woman, she does not know what to say.

"At least consider having more children," the woman shouts as she hurries off.

<u>*TRANSISTION (hereafter all will be bold and underlined)*</u>

<u>Thirteen years later</u>, the mother recalls the incident. "My daughter grew up an only child. She is fourteen years old now. She has turned out fine and not in spite of the fact that she is an only child. Because she is an only child, she has had benefits that other children do not have" (Carlson).

<u>Historically</u>, American society's misconceptions of only children are based on stereotypes and prejudice about the children and their parents. The stereotypes are false;

I.C. FUNCTIONAL INTRODUCTION

indeed, studies show that there are many positive benefits of being an only child. Being an only child has definite advantages. **Although** people commonly perceive[1] the only child as being spoiled, selfish, unhappy, and lonely, only children do not have any more social problems than the average child (Brophy 54). [2]Child psychology experts have been studying only children since the turn of the century. Extensive studies have shown that only children exhibit positive [3] personality traits not evident in children from larger families (Koontz 56). They score higher on [4]various tests of achievement and intelligence than do children with siblings. [5]Specific examples of only children illustrate the statistical evidence (Heil 102).

II. HISTORY OF NEGATIVE PERCEPTION

"Being an only child is a disease in itself." This was the conclusion of G. Stanley Hall, a prominent psychologist at the turn of the century (Kutner and Singer 109). One explanation for the popularity of Hall's theory is the fact that thirty of the first fifty doctoral students of psychology in the U.S. were instructed by him. Thus, his opinion became widely recognized as fact. This negative view of only children was accepted without question by psychologists for nearly seventy years (Sanders 25). *EXEMPLIFICATION OF STEREOTYPING* The disadvantaged children who were forced to spend life without siblings, psychologists concluded, were apt to be self-centered, unhappy, anxious, demanding, pampered, and maladjusted to the social world. Society has placed an invalid and unnecessary judgment on the only child (Goode 50).

Parents of only children are subject to almost as much false stereotyping as their offspring are. They have not escaped accusations of being neurotic and selfish, and of valuing material goods over children. They have also been criticized for raising a child in an inevitable detrimental environment (one without siblings) (Day 755). The problem with this distorted view of the only child is a far-reaching one. Overseas, particularly in English-speaking countries, only children are viewed as being "undesirable and . . . [having one is] fair neither to the child nor to the society" (755). There is no logical explanation behind this kind of thinking, other than simple ignorance (754).

CAUSE AND EFFECT RELATIONSHIP

In America, the image of the only child has reached such vast proportions as to actually influence the number of children couples have. **As Sanders points out,** in recent national surveys, a leading reason couples give for having another child is to prevent the first from being an only child (24). A **recent Gallup Poll** illustrates couples' fears of only children further. *PLACE OPPOSING EVIDENCE EARLY IN THE PAPER; THEN BURY IT WITH POSITIVE COUNTER-EVIDENCE.* An astounding 78 percent of Americans believe that only children are disadvantaged. Only five percent of the population thought that one child was ideal in 1986, up four percent since 1973. **On the contrary,** 59 percent of Americans regard the two-child family to be ideal (McGrath 19).

USE OF STATISTICS AND POLLS

Blake, a demographer at the University of California at Los Angeles, conducted a survey on American's feeling toward only children. Her conclusion: a vast majority of the Population see being an only child as a serious handicap. Over half believe only children possess negative personality traits. Approximately one-fourth consider only children lonely (210). **What is the irony of these surveys?** As Blake notes, "Only two percent of respondents believed, even when asked directly, that the major disadvantage suffered by only children is prejudice from teachers, neighbors, relatives, or other children" (19, 21).

III.CHILD STUDIES

"The view of only children as selfish and lonely is a gross exaggeration of reality," insists Falbo, a social psychologist at the University of Texas at Austin and leading expert on only children (Goode 50). This is welcome news for only children. The views of Hall and other psychologists of his time had been left unchallenged for more than half a century. It was not until about fifteen years ago that psychologists started to question these ideas (Kutner and Singer 100).

iV. POSITIVE PERSONALITY TRAITS and COMPARISON/CONTRAST

Probably the most common stereotype about children is that they are selfish. One assumes that since the only child never had any siblings to share with, he or she will be greedy by nature. **However,** quite the opposite is true. Being that they never had any negative experiences with sharing, the only child is unaccustomed to greediness and grabbing (Kiev and Sidar 46). *SCIENTIFIC RESEARCH FINDINGS* Society's misconceptions of only children are based on prejudice and stereotypes. Experts on only children stress the point over and over again: there is absolutely no scientific evidence to support the "pampered, lonely, misfit" theory. Thorough research on only children has yet to find the truth in these myths (Katz 199). The simplest explanation for spoiling in any family is the parents. A family of seven may be very wealthy **whereas** a family with only one child my be struggling to pay their bills on time. There are many other determining factors as to whether or not a child will be spoiled, including social class (Koontz 57).

COMPARISON/CONTRAST

The myths of the only child have been disproved by prominent psychologists repeatedly. **In the words of Blake,** "In study after study . . . [only children are] as advantaged, or more so, as children from two-child families, and clearly more advantaged than children from larger sib-sizes" (Day 755). **Among other things,** they receive a larger portion of their parents' income, they have no competition for parental attention, and have more time to themselves (755). *EXEMPLIFICATION* **Among the many beneficial aspects** of being an only child are the numerous positive personality traits unique to the only child. **For instance,** only children develop very close friendships. **In this way,** they develop very good social skills and an ability to communicate well with peers (Katz 199).

COMPARISON/CONTRAST Only children, in tests of sociability, actually fared better than children with siblings. They were rated well above the norm in these surveys of sociability, in terms of peer popularity or ratings by others. **One explanation** for only children's excellent social skills is the environment in which they are raised. Throughout childhood, they spend a great majority in the company of adults. **Through this one-on-one interaction,** they learn very mature social skills and superior communication skills (Polit and Falbo 312). Only children need to seek companionship from outside of the nuclear family. **As a result of this**, they are forced to become more "socially sophisticated," and are more likely to participate in extracurricular activities such as sports and student leadership (Kantrowitz and Greenburg 67). *COMPARISON/CONTRAST* It is not possible to gain exact results from this, but at a recent meeting of the American Psychological Association, members were asked to evaluate the happiness levels of only children. Their conclusion: only children are "as well or better adjusted" than other children in efficacy (which essentially means a sense of control over one's life). They consistently scored above average on these tests (Sanders 25).

Another area in which only children excel is leadership. Perhaps as a result of spending a lot of time alone and developing independence and self-reliance, only children are less likely to follow the crowd. Only children "tend to be not joiners, but leaders," observes Falbo (Polit and Falbo 25). *COMPARISON/CONTRAST* **One of the topics** rarely mentioned when discussing only children is the effect being raised without siblings has on a person in adult life. It is actually a rather positive one. In the workplace, only children choose careers that are "white-collar, scientific, and cerebral" as opposed to "blue-collar or manual operations." They also tend to marry better educated spouses and have fewer children. These facts are supported by the American Institute for Research's and survey of over 400,000 residents of Palo Alto, California (25).

EXEMPLIFICATION

Creativity is a strong characteristic in only children (25). Due to the fact that only children grow up without playmates in the nuclear family, they are often left to entertain themselves. Through this process of exploration or the imagination, only children are able to push their creative capabilities to the limits. **Often** being the only child makes the child constantly the center of attention, and parents and grandparents are frequent guests at the child's "productions." Many only children grow up to pursue careers in acting or art (Brophy 55).

EXAMPLE OF PARAPHRASE

AND COMPARISON/CONTRAST Prominent psychologist Falbo has concluded that the only child displays a great amount of character (which would include maturity and cooperativeness). **Because** only children receive more attention from their parents, psychologists hypothesize that they exhibit more character than those who receive less parental attention (Polit and Falbo).

EXAMPLE OF SUMMARY AND CAUSE AND EFFECT

Many things that are looked upon as being handicaps to the only child actually turn out in their favor. Receiving more parental attention, for instance, could result in higher self-confidence. Having their own bedroom does not foster loneliness, but instills independence and innovativeness. Being that all of the only child's friends come from outside the family, this could promote tolerance (Day 757).

V. ACHIEVEMENT COMPARISON/CONTRAST

Only children have an advantage over other individuals in academics, also. They tend to get slightly better grades, set higher goals for themselves, earn more advanced academic degrees, and show higher self-esteem (Koontz 56). The studies of Falbo and many other psychology experts show that only children score consistently higher on intelligence tests than do children from sibling groups. Many only children have skipped a grade or will skip a grade during the course of their education. **Even in 1953,** tests were being done to measure the intelligence levels of only children. In Scotland, when 10,000 children were studied, only children scored higher on these tests than did others (Sanders 25). *COMPARISON/CONTRAST* **The most significant difference** between children from sibling-groups and only children are the areas of self-esteem and achievement motivation. **In a number of studies,** only children have scored very high on these tests. Study after study have shown that they are extremely high achievers (Heil 102). On tests of verbal and quantitative ability, children without siblings scored consistently higher than the norm. **Between** 1960 and 1980, Claudy conducted some of the most important research on only children in the field. **Recently,** a study Claudy conducted compared 2,000 only children in high school with 2,000 children from two-child families. The only children scored slightly higher on the tests of verbal and quantitative ability (Kutner and Singer 110). Polit and Falbo recently reviewed hundreds of studies on academic achievement. They found a major gap between only children and the youngest children from larger families. The "onlies" had better grades, they had finished more school, and they were rated higher on tests of motivation (309).

<u>EXAMPLE OF SUMMARY</u>

A breakthrough study on only children was completed in 1989. This massive study of over 150,000 adults brought thrilling news for experts studying only children. It found that onlies are better educated and score higher on IQ tests than children from larger families. This study paved the way for more research. One particularly interesting study followed a few years later. In it, Blake found that, on average, children from one-child families receive twenty percent more education than the children from larger families do.

The research also proved that only children scored the highest on verbal IQ tests, which are an excellent indicator of future academic success. *EXAMPLE OF DIRECT QUOTE* "Every year, I ask my medical students how many are onlies or firstborns, and eighty-five percent of the class raise their hands," recounts child psychiatrist S. Kramer (Brophy 54).

<u>VI. SPECIFIC EXAMPLES</u>

<u>Although the positive aspects</u> of being an only child are very exciting and overwhelming, it is when they are put into real life situations that they are amazing to see. The creative spark that is commonly found in only children has ignited the flame of talent in many great artists. "Onlies have more of a sense of creating their own worlds than other kids," contends Slung, author of <u>The Only Child Book</u> (Brophy 54). A few of the more recognized artists and performers who were also only children are Ansel Adams, Ezra Pound, Lillian Hellman, John Updike, Truman Capote, Elvis Presley, Ingrid Bergman, Cary Grant, Frank Sinatra, and Leonardo da Vinci (54, 55).

<u>Obviously,</u> along with growing up an only child, comes spending a lot of time alone. This separation has proven beneficial to only children. Pediatrician Kappelman, who wrote <u>Raising the Only Child</u>, maintains that in large groups, only children "tend to dominate." Kappelman also observes that the first group of astronauts included a large number of only children (54).

The natural leadership skills that only children possess create outstanding opportunities for

only children in politics. Joseph Stalin, Indira Ghandi, and Franklin Delano Roosevelt (who was

raised an only child although he had a half-brother twenty-eight years older than he) are just a

few of the only children who took a stand for their beliefs in politics (54).

VII. CONCLUSION   THESIS RESTATED

Only children are not disadvantaged and lonely; indeed, the stereotypes and prejudice against

them are unfounded, and being brought up an "only" has many benefits. The experience

of being an only child is a special one. We are all, *NOTABLE QUOTE* as Shakespeare once said, "a part of

those whom we have met" (Sanders 25).

Works Cited

Brophy, Beth. "It Doesn't Hurt to be Alone." *U.S. News and World Report* 6 Mar. 1989:
54-55. Print.

Carlson, Joleen. Personal Interview. 11 Mar. 1996.

Day, Lincoln H. "Is There Any Socially Significant Psychological Difference in Being an
Only Child?: The Evidence from some Adult Behavior." *Journal of Applied Social
Psychology* 21.9 (1991): 754-774. Print.

Goode, Erica E. "Cracking the Myth of the Pampered, Lonely Misfit." *U.S. News and
World Report* 10 Jan. 1994: 50. *Ebscohost*. Web. 6 June 2009.

Heil, Andrea. "Raising the Unlonely Only Child." *Working Woman* July 1988: 102. Print.

Kantrowitz, Barbara and Nikki Finke Greenberg. "Only But Not Lonely." *Newsweek* 16
June 1986: 66-67. *LexisNexus*. Web. 28 Oct. 2008.

Katz, Lillian G. "The Only Child." *Parents* Dec. 1987: 190. Print.

Kiev, Ari and Alexander Sidar. *Breaking Free of Birth Order*. New York: Ballantine
Books, 1993. Print.

Koontz, Katy. "Only Children." *Utne Reader* May/June. 1994: 56. *LexisNexus*. Web. 20 Jan. 2009.

Kutner, Lawrence and Mark Singer. "Only Kids Aren't Lonely . . . ." *Parents* Feb. 1996:
109-110. *Ebscohost*. Web. 19 Dec. 2008.

McGrath, Ellie. *My One and Only*. New York: William Morrow and Company, 1989. Print. "Only
the Lonely." *Time* 13 May 1991: 54. Print.

Polit, Denise F. and Toni Falbo. "Only Children and Personality Development: A Quantitative
Review." *Journal of Marriage and the Family* 49.2 (1987): 309-326. Print.

Sanders, Jerry C. "Correcting the Myth of the Only Child." *USA Today* July 1995: 24. Print.

[For your information, Courtney Carlson, a Park High School graduate from Racine, Wisconsin,
won the Wisconsin State PTSA Reflections contest *twice*! She studied at Oxford College in
England. She grew up as an only child.]

INDEX